398.2
SHE

S0-BYC-337

30018000004263R

PAUL BUNYAN

AND HE WAS A GREAT LOGGER, THAT'S SURE—AND I GUESS THERE AIN'T
NOBODY PRETENDS THERE EVER WAS ANYBODY LIKE HIM . . .

PAUL BUNYAN

BY ESTHER SHEPHARD

Illustrated by Rockwell Kent

Harcourt Brace Jovanovich, Publishers

San Diego   New York   London

489 FOLLETT 4.31 7797

Copyright 1924, 1952 by Esther Shephard

Slightly Revised Edition

All rights reserved. No part of this publication may be reproduced or transmitted in any form or by any means, electronic or mechanical, including photocopy, recording, or any information storage and retrieval system, without permission in writing from the publisher.

Requests for permission to make copies of any part of the work should be mailed to: Permissions, Harcourt Brace Jovanovich, Publishers, Orlando, Florida 32887

Library of Congress Cataloging in Publication Data
Shephard, Esther.
  Paul Bunyan.
  Summary: A collection of exploits of the legendary lumberjack and his blue ox Babe.
  1. Bunyan, Paul (Legendary character)—Juvenile literature. [1. Bunyan, Paul (Legendary character)
2. Folklore—United States. 3. Tall tales]
I. Kent, Rockwell, 1882-1971, ill. II. Title.
PZ8.1.S5395Pau 1985   398.2'2'0973   85-5448
ISBN 0-15-259749-2
ISBN 0-15-259755-7 (pbk.)

Printed in the United States of America

T U V W
B C D E (pbk.)

CONTENTS

FULL PAGE ILLUSTRATIONS

INTRODUCTION

OST of these stories of Paul Bunyan have been collected from loggers in Washington, Oregon, and British Columbia, many of whom, of course, have followed the logging industry from the East, and have brought with them the stories as they were told in Canada, Michigan, and the middle-western logging section. In the camps these stories are usually told in competition, and some liberties, therefore, have been taken in arranging them in the form of a continuous narrative told by one logger; but I have tried always to keep as close to the originals as possible and substantially the stories are just as the men in the camps tell them.

The Paul Bunyan legend centers around a mythical hero of the woods, a kind of superlumberjack, who is noted for his wonderful deeds of cleverness and skill when some quick expedient is necessary and for the extraordinary size of his logging operations. Paul is never "stumped" and no job is ever too big or too hard for him and his Big Blue Ox to handle. The story of his deeds is really epic in its sweep and immensity, and his field of action covers practically all of America where the great forests have been.

It is rather difficult to say where these stories of Paul Bunyan began. Some evidence points to a French-Canadian origin among the loggers of Quebec or northern Ontario, who may even have brought them from the old country. But other evidences point just as strongly to an American beginning, possibly in Michigan or Wisconsin. Certainly the stories resemble those other frontier stories which were told in that time, back in the 30's and 40's, when western humor was at its height and when the most extravagant tales circulated, such, for instance, as those stories which were told of Davy Crockett. It is likely that part of this stream of western humor which filled such a large part of the literature of those early days, crowded out of the main channel by the excitement of the Civil War time, may have found its outlet in the logging camps in the great Northern Woods and turned itself naturally into the Paul Bunyan legends. Many of the tall tales of the early frontier have been taken over bodily and made into Paul Bunyan yarns.

The stories traveled westward as the logging industry traveled westward, and they seem to have been transformed to a considerable extent on the way. In the Minnesota camps, where the Scandinavian loggers were numerous, they were undoubtedly enriched by Scandinavian myth, and there Paul Bunyan assumed some of the characteristics of a modern Thor. Farther West the stories seem to have taken on a little coloring from local Indian legends. Just within the last few years a few of them have found their way into print, and advertising men of the large timber firms have used them in their literature with some freedom and often very skillfully. There are also some newer stories which branch out into other industries than that of logging.

In the old days when the stories were told around the comboose from the deacon seat there were men who could tell Paul Bunyan yarns evening after evening for weeks together and never repeat themselves, but now with the new conditions in the camps, with the advent of the story magazines and political tracts, and the newly awakened economic consciousness of the men, the center of interest has shifted, and the Paul Bunyan legends seem to be going into the discard, and there is some danger of their being allowed to die out. The oldest of the stories date back at least to the 1860's and perhaps even earlier, and they seem to have been at their height in the 80's and 90's.

The name "Paul Bunyan" in the camps (Bunyon it is spelled in the East and Bunion the French have it) has several different connotations. Sometimes it is merely a tag on which to hang a practical joke, sometimes it is the name of some particularly clumsy or awkward fellow among the loggers or some inefficient or particularly unpopular boss, and again sometimes it is the nickname given to some especially clever or skillful workman; but generally it refers to this mythical figure, Paul, who is the hero of the great adventures.

The teller almost always claims actual acquaintance with Paul. He "worked for him on the Big Onion," or "was with him the spring of the Round Drive," or "had a brother who drove the saleratus wagon for Paul," or "spent a winter in Paul's camp the year he logged three weeks this side of Quebec," or "used to court Paul's daughter Teeny," or "was one of the two thousand filers in Paul's shingle-mill," or something else equally substantiating. The stories are always told in perfect seriousness and there is sometimes a regular "code" which the narrator has to follow. He must tell the "truth."

For example: the dog that Paul Bunyan kept in his camp was not to feed the swampers to in the spring in order to get out of paying them wages, but to feed the watch peddlers, tailors' agents and camp inspectors to. And Paul Bunyan's Ox did not measure 42 axhandles between the eyes, but 42 axhandles and a tobacco box—"you could easy fit in a Star tobacco box after the last axhandle." The figures and dimensions given in the stories often vary with the audience. Usually the narrator "lays on all the traffic will bear," and whether a bridge is to be 14 or 400 feet wide depends somewhat on the character of the person to whom the story is told. Very generally the stories contain some sly irony or humor at the expense of the "boss."

An obvious use of the stories is, naturally, to string the tenderfoot or to put a smart-Alec in his proper place. If someone comes to camp who brags of the big logs they took out in the camp where he last worked it is not long before he is "taken down a peg" by a Paul Bunyan yarn, and the greenhorn has always to be put through a number of practical jokes. The logging industry, of course, is not unique in this respect. Almost every industry has its own peculiar trade stories and its stock practical jokes to pull off on the uninitiated. If it isn't the hodag and the crosshaul it is the left-handed monkey-wrench or the red oil to fill the red lantern on the caboose.

The stories in this volume have been selected from a great number and do not include stories which are too technical or too closely tied up with some small geographic detail to be of general interest, and stories which in my opinion seemed to be too new or too far outside the pale really to belong to the Paul Bunyan cycle. Where there have been several versions of the same story the one which seemed the most interesting has been chosen or the one which best fitted into the plan of the book. Since the stories are so numerous, I am sure there must be a great many that I have not heard, and I should be glad to have any such stories sent to me. The Paul Bunyan legend, the unique contribution of the American frontier to the world's folk-lore, certainly deserves to be preserved.

ESTHER SHEPHARD

Shepherd's Bush,
Suquamish, Washington.

PAUL BUNYAN

PAUL'S CRADLE

F WHAT they say is true Paul Bunyan was born down in Maine. And he must of been a pretty husky baby too, just like you'd expect him to be, from knowin' him afterwards.

When he was only three weeks old he rolled around so much in his sleep that he knocked down four square miles of standin' timber and the goverment got after his folks and told 'em they'd have to move him away.

So then they got some timbers together and made a floatin' cradle for Paul and anchored it off Eastport, but every time Paul rocked in his cradle, if he rocked shoreward, it made such a swell it come near drownin' out all the villages on the coast of Maine, and the waves was so high Nova Scotia come pretty near becomin' an island instead of a peninsula.

And so that wouldn't do, of course, and the goverment

got after 'em again and told 'em they'd have to do somethin'
about it. They'd have to move him out of there and put him
somewheres else, they was told, and so they figgured they'd
better take him home again and keep him in the house for a
spell.

But it happened Paul was asleep in his cradle when they
went to get him, and they had to send for the British navy
and it took seven hours of bombardin' to wake him up. And
then when Paul stepped out of his cradle it made such a swell
it caused a seventy-five foot tide in the Bay of Fundy and
several villages was swept away and seven of the invincible
English warships was sunk to the bottom of the sea.

Well, Paul got out of his cradle then, and that saved Nova
Scotia from becomin' an island, but the tides in the Bay of
Fundy is just as high as they ever was.

And so I guess the old folks must of had their hands full
with him all right. And I ought to say, the king of England
sent over and confiscated the timbers in Paul's cradle and
built seven new warships to take the place of the ones he'd
lost.

When Paul was only seven months old he sawed off the
legs from under his dad's bed one night.

The old man noticed when he woke up in the mornin' that
his bed seemed considerable lower than it used to be, and so
he got up and investigated, and, sure enough, there was the
legs all sawed off from under it and the pieces layin' out
on the floor.

And then he remembered he'd felt somethin' the night
before, but he'd thought he must be dreamin'—the way you
do dream that you're fallin' down sometimes when you first

THEY HAD TO SEND FOR THE BRITISH NAVY

go off to sleep.

And he looked around to see who could of done it and there was Paul layin' there sound asleep with his dad's crosscut saw still held tight in his fist and smilin' in his sleep as pretty as anythin'.

And he called his wife and when she come in he says to her:

"Did you feel anythin' in the night?" he says.

"No," she says. "Is anythin' wrong?"

"Well, just look here," he says. And he showed her the four-by-eights layin' there on the floor and the saw in the kid's hand.

"I didn't light the lamp when I went to get up this mornin'," she says, "and I guess I didn't notice it."

"Well, it's Paul's done it," the old man says. "And I'll bet that boy of ourn is goin' to be a great logger some day. If he lives to grow up he's goin' to do some great loggin' by and by, you just see—a whole lot bigger than any of the men around here has ever done."

And they was right, all right. There ain't never been loggin' before nor since like Paul Bunyan done.

And then they tell another story about Paul when he was a little kid too that's pretty good, about how he killed some wild animals one day.

Paul was out crawlin' one time, before he'd learned to walk yet, out in his father's clearin'—about forty acres or so around the house till you got to the edge of the timber. His ma wasn't watchin' him very close and it wasn't long before Paul was right up to the edge of them woods. Among other things that he'd picked up and was holdin' in his hand was a long pole that his father'd used for a leever for grubbin' stumps; for Paul'd been crawlin' around, like babies will, pickin' round in things, and playin' in the grass and stumps, and just pickin' up and holdin' onto almost anythin' that happened to come handy.

And, like I said, he'd got right out to the edge of them woods, and was holdin' onto that pole he had.

The woods them days was full of all kinds of wild animals —bears, wolves, cougars, snakes, coons, moose, and all kinds of things, and there was lots of 'em too and they wasn't afraid of nothin'. With so few people around they wasn't no more afraid of men than they was of anything else.

And so when Paul was sittin' there with his pole like that, the first thing that come onto him was a big moose that some hunter'd taken a shot at and hurt him, but hadn't killed him, but just made him awful mad, and of course he was goin' to go right on the boy, because a moose when he's been hurt that way just tries to kill the first human he sees after that, and he was makin' right straight for Paul with his horns down.

But Paul happened to be holdin' the pole out and what happened was, the moose run right onto that and split himself clean through from stem to stern and stuck on the pole so that just his little tail was layin' out behind along the pole, and of course, pinned tight that way, he couldn't hurt Paul none.

And then next a cougar come along and he was goin' to make a spring for the kid, I guess, but midway he got his claws and tail all tangled up in the moose's horns and was held tight in his place.

Well, then comes a timber wolf. He was goin' to try to sneak around the cougar and get at Paul, but the cougar wasn't dead yet and took a bite in his neck and got lock-jaw and couldn't let go, and so the wolf was settled for.

And then next to come was a coon.

He must of come paddin' along the pole expectin' to jump over the heads of the others, I spose, and get at Paul that way. He must of had his tail hangin' down and been just at the end of the pole, and the way it looked afterwards Paul must of give the pole a poke about that time, for when they found 'em I'll be blamed if the pole hadn't gone through every ring of the coon's tail and hadn't missed a one and was holdin' him fast, or just about—a bull-snake had got himself tied around the end of the pole to keep any of the rings from slippin' off.

And so when his ma found him, there he was, sittin' on the ground with all them critters squirmin' on the stick in his hand.

"Goo, goo!" he says, and kind of grunted—like as if he was tryin' to tell her that the mess of 'em was too heavy for him to crawl back to the house and carry it with him, or otherwise he would of been in before now to get his supper.

Course it never occurred to him that he might of let go— babies always holds onto things so—and then maybe he was afraid that the snake might get untied again if he let go the pole and the coon and the other ones might slip off.

Anyway he was holdin' onto it good and tight and had 'em all safe.

Tom Larkin told this story, I remember, one night when we was all spinnin' yarns, just after somebody else had just

told one about some other kid, and Tom's story sure made
the first fellow's story look pretty sick, I can tell you. And I
don't doubt but what Tom had the facts, though he didn't
say just where this happened, whether it was in Maine or
some other place where Paul was livin' at the time.

Paul Bunyan always seemed like a real Michigan man to
me, and I never could get used to his bein' born back in
Maine; but it always seemed to me as if he should of been
born and raised right there in Michigan. But I spose maybe
that's because I first went to work for him there, and that's
where I knowed him first, and it always seemed to me as if
he belonged there. But that ain't nothin', of course. He'd
logged for a good many winters before I met him, one season
on the Porcupine, I know, and the followin' winter three
weeks this side of Quebec. And he logged on the Ottawa
after I went to work for him, and some say he'd been there
before, when he first started out, and that that's where he
come from the very first—started in loggin' in some French
settlement up there. I don't know. The story about that he
was born down in Maine a man from Maine himself told
me. McDowell his name was. Him and his son was both of
'em in camp together, same time I was, and same camp for a
good many years, in the old days. It was the young fellow
told me the story about Paul. The old man used to wear a
red check mackinaw, I remember, and had awful heavy eye-
brows—about the thickest I ever seen—long and bushy, that
stood straight out, and used to get full of frost in the winter.

Fine old chap he was, though.

They used to tell how Paul went to school part of a day
when he was a kid, back in Maine. His father and mother

got him a slate—cleaved out of a mountain-side in Vermont
—and a pencil imported from Germany that would be big
enough for him, and then they sent him to school to learn
to read, and write, and cipher. The schoolmaster was an old
man whose mother lived to be over a hundred years old.

Well, the first thing the teacher started Paul in on was to
write the figgurs, "1, 2, 3, 4," on his slate, and Paul grabbed
his slate pencil and went to work.

He was tryin' his best to make the curlycues just right,
but the figgurs was so big that all the lines looked straight to
the old man, who couldn't only see but part of 'em at a time.
And so he got mad at Paul, and I don't know what he was
goin' to try to do to him, but anyway Paul picked him up
and throwed him in the stove—it was one of them big ones
they used to have in the middle of the room in them old-time
schoolhouses.

And then Paul started for the door. But he tripped on the
stove and knocked it over, and the stove-door come open, and
the old man got out, and took after Paul.

Well, Paul kept a-goin' up the road as hard as he could
leg it with his breath comin' out in puffs like the exhaust of
an ocean liner and freezin' all around him—for it was a cold
November day. He'd left the old schoolmaster miles behind
at the start, but he was goin' so hard he couldn't stop, and
kept right on goin' over hill and down dale, like they say
in the song, till he got pretty near to the Gulf of St.
Lawrence.

Then he stopped, and quit puffin' so hard, but them frost
breaths of his that froze trailin' behind him that cold November day is still hangin' round the Maine coast. Sometimes

they get out to sea and then they're called fog, and they hang around the big icebergs, and the big ships get lost in 'em and get on the rocks and ice, like the *Titanic* done.

Of course Paul was big for his age, but he wasn't clumsy like some big boys. He was so quick he could catch a squirrel on the frame of a barn, or he could stand in the middle of the floor and jump and plant both feet flat on the ceilin', and some of the old Maine loggers tell how he could blow out the bunkhouse light and get in his bunk before it was dark.

And at loggin' he was A-1 right from the start, I guess, for they say he cut his teeth on a peavey and drove logs down the Kennebec in his first pair of pants. He went to work for his uncle up in Ontario when he was still just a kid, and because he was so much quicker and bigger and stronger than any of the men even then, they used to give him several jobs that nobody else in camp could do. One job he had was day-breaker. The cook used to send him up in the Blue Mountains with an ax to break day and Paul was so quick he could always get his job done and get back to camp and call the men to breakfast long before the daylight got there. And another job he had was blowin' the dinnerhorn for the cook. When Paul'd blow, the noise was always so loud the men could ride in out of the woods on the echo.

I ain't never surprised to hear anythin' like that about Paul when he was a kid from them that knowed him then, for I know he must of been a great kid to grow to be the kind of logger he was. And he was a great logger, that's sure— and I guess there ain't nobody pretends there ever was any-body like him.

I remember in the old time when we used to be gettin' out squared timbers for the British trade how Paul used to go out a half mile in the woods and begin squarin' the trees up.

Four cuts was all Paul ever made to a tree—one on each side and it was done. And he'd work a half hour or so, and then when he'd get 'em all standin' like that clean and white, he'd get his ax on the wove grass handle and swing it around and cut 'em all down, a third of an acre at a time, and hitch the Blue Ox to 'em and snake 'em down to the river, and they'd float away, a raft fourteen miles long of clean, white timbers. Course squared timbers always floats on their edge, and that made it a plaguy hard job to stick on 'em when we had to drive 'em down the river, the way we used to, down the Ottawa in the old time. The British buyers was mighty partikkelar and didn't want 'em marked up with shoe calks nor nothin', but Paul knowed what to do about that all right. What he done was, he just had the calks took out of the men's shoes and put in the timbers instead, and got wooden shoes for the men to wear on the drive, and that way they never got 'em cut up so bad.

I logged for Paul for a good many years, and it was fine loggin' too them old times. Not like it is now. When the trees used to be standin' tall and thick so that the only way you could look was straight up, and all you could see was a little patch of blue right above you, and all you could smell was the smell of the firs and balsam and pine around you, and all you could hear was the squirrels and chickadees, and the scrape of the lumberjacks' saws and the bite of their axes. That was fine loggin'. Not like the measly little stump tracts we got here now to log, with small scraggly trees and lonesome-lookin' burnt trunks standin' around. You can't log in that there kind of country.

THE CAMP
⇝ ON ⇝
THE BIG ONION

HE time I first went to work for Paul was the winter he was loggin' on the Big Onion.

I'd been workin' for old man Gilroy for a good many winters and then finally when he went broke, I thought here's my chance to go to work for Paul. I'd been hearin' about him, of course, for he'd been loggin' on Smith's Neck, down Lake Erie way, a year or two before that and on the Little Gimlet where it empties into the Big Auger, and so when I heard he was up on the Big Onion that fall I went up there to go to work for him—there wasn't hardly a logger in Michigan but what was workin' for Paul that winter. The only job Paul had to give me was helper to the stable-boss to start with, for the first couple of months, but then afterwards I was one of the regular fallers.

It was sure a tough job, that first job I had, and I never

wanted it again, for Bill, of course, like always, was takin'
care of the Blue Ox; and he was an awful animal to take
care of. It seems sometimes we was out pretty near all night
workin' away with that critter, for naturally I was supposed
to be helpin' Bill, though he didn't really want me and kind
of told Paul so after a while, I guess, and so Paul put me
on with the woods gang. But then, even if it was tough, bein'
out early that way give me the chance to see the men comin'
down for their hotcakes in the mornin', and I guess maybe
that was worth somethin'—I know I wouldn't of missed it
for a good deal. And then it give me the chance to get ac-
quainted a little bit with Babe too, and kind of give me the
run of things at camp.

Paul's camp was so big it was kind of hard for me to
get used to it at first—for I hadn't had no experience with
loggin' on that kind of a scale—till after a while I kind of
learned to find my way around between the buildin's and
teamsters and cattle and cooks and everybody.

The number of men in Paul's camp was never correctly
counted that I know of, for there was always too many
there, and too many goin' out and comin' in all the time
for anyone ever to be able to count 'em. But one time Paul
made a kind of an estimate for a report he had to make to
the goverment. They'd asked for figgurs and he said he'd
try to get 'em for 'em.

So then he told the chief clerk to count 'em up but after
he'd been tryin' for a couple of weeks, runnin' around all
over, Johnny come back and told him it couldn't be done.

"There's too many goin' and comin' all the time," he says.

"Well, count the cattle, then," Paul says. "I know there's

about five men for every yoke of cattle. That's what I always figgur on anyway. You can give 'em the report on that."

And, "Go on," he says to Windy, who was turnin' the grindstone for him that day, behind the cook-house, where he was sharpenin' up his ax.

But Johnny didn't have no better luck countin' the cattle, for they was goin' and comin' too, and there was a lot of 'em and some of 'em was always bein' killed off for the cook every meal and new ones comin' in from the stockyards.

And so in a couple of days he come up to Paul again and he says, "I can't count 'em, Paul."

That time Paul was just startin' down the road with the Blue Ox to take some logs down to the landin', and I know he didn't like to stop, but he did, though, for just a minute.

"Whoa, Babe!" he hollers.

"I tell you what," he says to Johnny, "pile up the yokes and measure 'em, and figgur from that. It won't be just exactly right, but it'll have to do. We can't waste any plaguy more time with it. We got loggin' to do." And he went on down the road.

And so Johnny, the chief clerk, got the straw boss and some of the rest of us to help him, and we went out there and piled the yokes up, and when we got it done we measured 'em and found we had just exactly three hundred and seventy cords. Figgurin' so many to the cord, and then five men to each yoke, like Paul had said, Johnny could make up the figgurs that was sent in to the goverment.

But of course then that was countin' only about one-third of 'em. In Paul's camp was where the three-shift system was invented, and so we always had one shift in camp, one goin' out to work and one out in the woods, and by measurin' the yokes that way you couldn't only get but one-third of 'em at a time, naturally.

That first fall I was workin' for Paul was when he got the big hotcake griddle. Always in the woods in them days the boys was mighty fond of hotcakes—just like men are pretty generally anywheres, I guess—and if there was anything could be said for Paul it was that he tried to treat his men right. And so, naturally, he wanted 'em to have hotcakes if there was any way he could fix it, and then besides, the way he ate 'em afterwards, he was more'n a little fond of 'em himself.

Well, in camp before that they hadn't never had hotcakes, because they didn't have no griddle big enough to cook 'em on, and no stove they could of put the griddle on if they'd of had it anyway, and so what they had for breakfast before that and what they was havin' when I went to work for Paul was just sourdough biscuits. And even so the cook used to have to get up twenty-six hours before daylight to get the biscuits cooked in time because all he had to cook 'em on was one of them there drumhead stoves they used to have and he couldn't only cook but sixty-four drippin' pans full at a time.

But that year Paul made up his mind he was goin' to have hotcakes for the men and he was goin' to have a griddle big enough to cook 'em on. And so he went down to the plow-works at Moline, Illinois, and contracted for 'em to make him one to suit him.

The steel that went into this griddle of Paul's was what would of gone into two hundred and sixty breakin' plows,

AND HERE SHE COME, ROLLIN' RIGHT ALONG

and when it was done finally, it measured two hundred and thirty-five foot across.

And then the men at the plow-works, of course, didn't have no way to ship it up to Paul and they was out there in the yard at the works figgurin' on how they could build some side-tracks and put several flatcars alongside each other and try to ship it up on them, when Paul happened to come along to see if his griddle wasn't finished yet.

"Never mind that," he says to the men when he seen 'em out there. "Never mind tryin' to build any extra tracks. We couldn't never get enough cars anyway, I don't believe. I'll just raise 'er up on edge and hitch my Blue Ox to 'er, and she'll roll right along."

And so after they'd got out of the way he raised 'er up, and hitched on, and started right out for home.

And when he come to within four or five miles of the camp, like he'd calculated it out beforehand, I guess, he just unhitched the Blue Ox and let the griddle spin on by itself. And here she come, rollin' right along. And when she got to just the right place, where he'd figgured to place her, she begun to spin round and round like spin-the-plate at a play-party and dug a nice big hole for the fire to go in under it, and settled right down and was all ready to go.

Paul had the bull-cooks pile in an acre or two of brush for a good fire, and him and Ole the Blacksmith rigged up a tank for the cook to make his batter in and a flume with a stop-cock in it, so's he could run it out onto the griddle and then shut it off whenever he had enough. Paul got flunkies with slabs of bacon strapped to their feet to skate around on the griddle to keep it greased, and a chicken wire fence all

around for 'em to climb up on when the batter come in too
thick. We rigged up a kind of block and tackle arrangement
to haul the hotcake off with when it was done—that's on that
first griddle. Afterwards, like in the camp in North Dakota,
Paul, of course, always had donkey engines.

There was four hundred bull-cooks bringin' in the spruce-
boughs for the bunks in the big bunkhouse at that first camp
I was in; it had eighty tiers of bunks, most of 'em muzzle
loaders but the two bottom layers, they was sidewinders. And
the men used to go to bed in balloons at night and come down
in parachutes in the mornin'.

A pretty sight it used to be to watch 'em comin' down.

"R-o-oo-ool out! Daylight in the swamp!" one of the
cookees would yell, and then in a minute or two they'd all
be rollin' out of their blankets, and the parachutes would
open and they'd all come sailin' down. It sure was a pretty
sight—about as fine a show as I ever laid eyes on.

Sometimes in the mornin' I used to stop at the door of the
bunkhouse, on my way from the barn, to watch 'em. For Bill
and I generally used to be on our way in to breakfast about
that time, and Bill'd sometimes take the time to stop for a
minute or so.

"I like to see 'em," he'd say to me. "Angus, that's a mighty
fine show. They come faster now than they used to when it
was just for sourdough biscuits. But we'll have to hustle along
and get our hotcakes. We got to get back to the Ox."

That spring on the Big Onion we had an awful lot of
trouble with the garlic that growed there where Garlic Crick
joins the Big Onion River—a kind of V-shaped tract in there
along the loggin' road, that was just full of it. The cook tried

to use it all up seasonin' the soup but the Frenchies wouldn't
stand for it in their pea-soup after the first week, and even
with that he only got the top layer off and then there was
four more layers growin' under that one. It beats all how
thick that wild garlic can grow when it gets a good start.
Everybody that even went by that place was seasoned so strong
there wasn't nobody else could live with him and, worst of

it, he couldn't stand to live with himself even. And we pretty
near just had to break up camp, but then Paul heard that the
Italian garlic crop was goin' to fail that year and so we
grubbed up the whole piece, every last layer of it, and shipped
it all to Italy and that way we got rid of it at last; just in
time when a good many of us was goin' on the drive anyway, though.

THE
PYRAMID FORTY

OME good loggin' that Paul done when I was with him was a couple of years after that on the Pyramid Forty, the same year we'd had the Long Rain the spring before. There wasn't only one forty of land there—by goverment surveys anyhow—but Paul got over 246,000,000 feet of timber off that one forty before the season was over. And the reason was, it was shaped like a pyramid—so high it took a man a week to see the top, or seven men could do it in a day if they all looked together. That way there was room for a lot of timber on it—a good deal more'n the goverment surveyors figgured there would be, and a whole lot more'n they ever knowed come off of it, that's sure.

But of course it was a tough job buildin' camp so much on the slope.

"You can't build a camp on the level on any such slope as that," Paul says.

But he figgured around for a while and it wasn't long till he'd got it all calculated out and a lot of new improvements along with it that would take advantage of the lay of the country.

What he done was, he built the camp down in a little hollow first that had a slope up the other way, and then afterwards he turned it around and put it up on the pyramid—kind of near the foot—not too far up. The bunkhouse and barns was down below and the cook-shack and commissary hung out over the top.

And loggin' on the side-hill wasn't so bad neither when you got used to it. The way we took the logs out, naturally, goin' up on one side and down on the other, in the long run it come to about the same as if we'd been workin' on level ground all the time anyway.

And it made it pretty handy in a good many ways. For one thing, the boys used to keep their axes sharp by goin' up to the top of the pyramid and pressin' the edge against one of the big rocks up there and start it rollin' downhill and keep runnin' after it, holdin' onto their ax-handle. That way it come in pretty good for 'em, especially after double-jaw Murphy'd chawed up the camp grindstone one night walkin' in his sleep, and Paul hadn't been able to get another one yet.

In the bunkhouse the bunks was all on swivels, and bein' on a slant like that, they'd get worked round by mornin', of course, so it made 'em pretty handy to roll out of. And in the cook-house the grub could always be sent down the tables by gravity.

SO HIGH IT TOOK A MAN A WEEK TO SEE THE TOP

The men that drove the watertanks over the ice-roads at night didn't have to drive all the way but could just let the water down from the top. And for helpin' the knotters to trim the branches off the trees, the sawyers'd just fall 'em downhill, and they'd stick in the ground and stand up that way so you could get at 'em easier. But of course sometimes that wasn't no advantage, because we wouldn't always know it was the same tree, if we was workin' fast, and that way one tree'd maybe get cut down several times before it got to the bottom of the forty.

But it was generally all right though. And I reckon the boys would of learned a whole lot more ways of usin' the side-hill methods if we'd of stayed longer, but Paul didn't stay only that one winter. I knowed a man once that logged on the same forty for five years runnin', but that wasn't Paul, not while I was with him anyway, though he might of made a long loggin' like that before my time with him. The old lumbermen used to do that. It saved 'em movin' around, of course, or havin' to buy up any more land from the goverment.

There was only one—or, well, yes, two, countin' one of the straw bosses—that really got adopted to side-hill loggin' in that one winter. That was the boss that took his job so hard he thought he had to watch everybody at the same time, and used to wear out both his shoes on the inside runnin' about such a lot, till he got the idea of takin' 'em off and changin' 'em to the other foot at noon every day; and so he saved his shoes that way. And then the other one was a little flunky we had that used to carry the lunch to the men in the woods when they was workin' too far out to come in to camp at noon. He had to skirt round the side-hill so much that he wore off one leg shorter'n the other, but it was a good thing, for then when he got it wore down he could get around without spillin' the coffee or the soup no more.

Course he didn't have to carry no lunch to the Frenchmen. If he had of, he'd probly of had two short legs instead of one. The Frenchmen, as I suppose everybody knows, always carried soup in their peavey handles. All they ever wanted was just pea-soup anyway, and they put that in hot every morning in holes they'd bored in their peavey handles. The friction of their hands workin' up and down on the handles kept the soup nice and hot till noon. Paul always liked the Frenchmen on account of that. He used to hire a good many—sometimes pretty near all the men in camp was French, and they was mighty good loggers, too, and good story tellers, most of 'em.

In many ways that year on the Pyramid Forty was one of the most interestin' winters I ever put in with Paul. There was some mighty queer animal creatures lived there on the forty, for one thing. One of 'em was the Pinnacle Grouse, and another one was the side-hill dodger, or Side-Hill Gouger— they was called that sometimes. They must of lived there a good long time, I should say, from the way they'd adopted themselves to the lay of the land.

The Pinnacle Grouse had only one wing—and that was a big one, which she always managed to keep on the outside when flyin' around. She frequented the top of the Pyramid mostly—you could see 'em almost always on sunny days flyin' in flocks against the sky near the highest point of the Pyramid. She was a pretty bird—a kind of brown, with yellow stripes on her head and breast—three yellow stripes in the middle of the forehead, then a blue, and a yellow, and then two yellows, and on her breast long yellow ones, on one side extendin' out to the edge of the wing, and little narrow blue stripes runnin' out along the feathers of the big wing and back onto the tail. Very pretty markin's when you saw her close, and she was sure pretty off at a distance in flight. With one wing big that way she could fly round and round in little circles or big circles, which ever she liked, but of course, anyone might know, she never could go straight ahead—not the way she was built. The one wing was bound to carry her round and round. And then of course she could go up and down if she wanted, though she didn't hardly ever want to do that. They generally hung around pretty close to the top, circlin' about the very highest tip of the Pyramid, where they could take a bath in the clouds if they wanted to, and then come down to roost on the telephone poles and other trees growin' up there.

The side-hill dodger wasn't a bird like the grouse, he was more like a coon or a woodchuck, kind of a cross between a coon and a woodchuck, though he didn't have rings like a coon, on his tail—but he was like a bird because they laid eggs, something like some of them Australian animals that you hear 'em tell about. He was kind of gray and brown, and black all over, and had all four feet black, except one generally. He was made so he had two long legs on the downhill side and two short legs on the uphill side—that's how well he had adopted himself to livin' on the side-hill.

And the hen dodgers always laid square eggs to keep 'em from rollin' down out of the nest she made. But one time it happened one of the mother dodgers had laid her eggs wrong side to, and then when the little dodgers come out they had their long legs on the uphill side and their short legs on the downhill side, and they all rolled down to the river at the bottom of the Forty and was drowned.

A crowd of us was standin' right there at the time watchin' 'em, but they was goin' so fast there wasn't nothing we could do to stop 'em. That was the only case I ever knowed of where the mother dodgers laid 'em wrong, I think. But we sure hated to see 'em drowned that time, because we was all fond of the little dodgers, and used to like to watch 'em playin' round in the woods when they was little and just learnin' to walk.

And then—well, then there was the hodag of course—that was an animal you found in most any of the camps back there and not only on the Pyramid Forty, but most any place.

The hodag wasn't so bad, but he could make the most awful noise—the worst you ever heard. Something between a screech and a growl, that wasn't neither, but both of 'em together at the same time, and a whole lot of other things throwed in besides. You'd think a whole woodsfull of wild-cats and hyenas was after you when you heard one of 'em.

And he wasn't pretty to look at neither when you seen him by himself—especially if you was by yourself too. With horns on the back of his legs like a rooster's only twelve hundred times as big, and long claws that turned under kind of and had big barbs on 'em up a little ways from the points, and big spikes all along his back that they said he could throw when he got mad like a porcupine throws his quills, only much more speed, and then, finally, stiff hair all over his body that had somethin' in it so it burned you when you got close to it, like nettles.

He was sure a bad one, and enough to scare anybody out
of their skins at first, I should say—specially the greenhorns
who'd just come to camp. They was generally all awful scared
of the hodag the first few weeks, but after they'd been in
camp awhile and hadn't seen none, only heard 'em, they generally got over bein' scared—most of 'em anyway—the same
as they did with the traveau too. Everybody but Buttermilk
Gibson. They had old Gibson sittin' on the barn roof all night
with a shotgun, to see that the hodag didn't carry off the
straw boss's cow that he kept in a shed at camp.

And then there was another animal that lived on the Pyramid Forty and that was a fierce creature that was called the
Ring-tailed Bavalorous.

He wasn't queer or peculiar like the other ones, but only
fierce and ornery, and he hung out generally pretty well down
by the bottom of the Forty, layin' in wait for the swampers
or a team of cattle comin' home late at night. He was a terrible animal when he got mad, and he was pretty hard to kill.
Only Paul once in a while would get one, and that wasn't
so very many times neither.

One time it happened that Babe the Blue Ox finished up
one of 'em all by himself once, and did a pretty good job of
it too.

Babe was comin' along down the loggin' road one evenin'
and the Ring-tailed Bavalorous was sittin' out on a limb of a
tree waitin' for him, ready to spring on him when he'd come
under the tree. They was so fierce, the bavalorous was, and so
reckless, they didn't care who they tackled, even Babe. He
calculated to jump down on him, I suppose, and scratch his

eyes out, and blind him. Anyway Babe seen him in time, and that stopped it, for just when the bavalorous was comin' sailin' down through the air ready to land on his nose, Babe just turned his head over a little to one side, and he landed on his horn and split himself clean through to his back. Then pretty soon when he was sure that he'd got him all right, Babe swung his head over and shook him off of that horn and onto the other horn, so he got another hole through him, and then that's the way he kept it up, until that fierce bavalorous looked like a piece of beefsteak that the cook had pounded holes through with his meat hammer, and there was nothin' much but his ringed tail left.

Babe come into camp that night with the remains of the bavalorous hangin' over his left horn that way and the tail skewed down over his left eye. And then some of us took the carcass off of him, and the bull-cook cut off the tail and used it to sweep the ashes out from under the big heatin' stove that winter.

BABE THE BLUE OX

PAUL BUNYAN couldn't of done all the great loggin' he did if it hadn't been for Babe the Blue Ox. I believe I mentioned helpin' to take care of him for a couple of months when I first come to camp, and then I helped measure him once afterwards for a new yoke Ole had to make for him. He'd broke the one he had when Paul was doin' an extra quick job haulin' lumber for some mill-men down in Muskegon one summer, and Ole had to make him a new one right away and so we had to take Babe's measurements.

I've forgot most of the other figgurs, but I remember he measured forty-two axhandles between the eyes—and a to-bacco box—you could easy fit in a Star tobacco box after the last axhandle. That tobacco box was lost and we couldn't never take the measurements again, but I remember that's what it was. And he weighed accordin'. Though he never was weighed that I know of, for there never was any scales made that would of been big enough.

Paul told Ole he might as well make him a new log chain too while he was at it, for the way Babe pulled on 'em, in just about a month or two what had been a chain would be pulled out into a solid bar and wouldn't be any good. And so we measured him up for the chain too.

Babe was so long in the body, Paul used to have to carry a pair of field glasses around with him so as he could see what he was doin' with his hind feet.

One time Babe kicked one of the straw bosses in the head, so his brains all run out, but the cook happened to be handy and he filled the hole up with hotcake batter and plastered it together again and he was just as good as ever. And right now, if I'm not mistaken, that boss is runnin' camp for the Bigham Loggin' Company of Virginia, Minnesota.

Babe was so big that every time they shod him they had to open up a new iron mine on Lake Superior, and one time when Ole the Blacksmith carried one of his shoes a mile and a half he sunk a foot and a half in solid rock at every step.

His color was blue—a fine, pretty, deep blue—and that's why he was called the Blue Ox—when you looked up at him the air even looked blue all around him. His nose was pretty near all black, but red on the inside, of course, and he had big white horns, curly on the upper section—about the upper third—and kind of darkish brown at the tip, and then the rest of him was all that same deep blue.

He didn't use to be always that blue color though. He was white when he was a calf. But he turned blue standin' out in the field for six days the first winter of the Blue Snow, and he never got white again. Winter and summer he was always the same, except probly in July—somewheres about the Fourth—he might maybe've been a shade lighter then.

I've heard some of the old loggers say that Paul brought him from Canada when he was a little calf a few days old— carried him across Lake Champlain in a sack so he wouldn't have to pay duty on him. But I'm thinkin' he must of been a mighty few days old at the time or Paul couldn't of done it, for he must of grown pretty fast when he got started, to grow to the size he did. And then besides there's them that says Paul never had him at all when he was a little fellow like that, but that he was a pretty fair-sized calf when Paul got him. A fellow by the name of O'Regan down near Detroit is supposed to of had him first. O'Regan didn't have no more'n about forty acres or so under cultivation cleared on his farm and naturally that wasn't near enough to raise feed for Babe, and so he's supposed to of sold him the year of the Short Oats to Paul Bunyan. I don't know exactly. It's all before my time. When I went to work for Paul, and all the time I knowed him, the Ox was full grown.

Babe was as strong as the breath of a tote-teamster, Paul always said, and he could haul a whole section of timber with him at a time—Babe'd walk right off with it—the entire six hundred forty acres at one drag, and haul it down to the landin' and dump it in. That's why there ain't no section thirty-seven no more. Six trips a day six days a week just cleaned up a township, and the last load they never bothered to haul back Saturday night, but left it lay on the landin' to float away in the spring, and that's why there quit bein' section 37's, and you never see 'em on the maps no more.

The only time I ever saw Babe on a job that seemed to nearly stump him—but that sure did look like it was goin' to for a while, though—durin' all the time I was with Paul was one time in Wisconsin, down on the St. Croix. And that was when he used him to pull the crooks out of eighteen miles of loggin' road; that come pretty near bein' more'n the Ox could handle. For generally anything that had two ends to it Babe could walk off with like nothin'.

But that road of all the crooked roads I ever see—and I've seen a good many in my day—was of all of 'em the crookedest, and it's no wonder it was pretty near too much for Babe. You won't believe me when I tell you, but it's the truth, that in that stretch of eighteen miles that road doubled back on itself no less than sixteen times, and made four figure 8's, nine 3's, and four S's, yes, and one each of pretty near every other letter in the alphabet.

Of course the trouble with that road was, there was too much of it, and it didn't know what to do with itself, and so it's no wonder it got into mischief.

You'd be walkin' along it, all unsuspectin', and here of a sudden you'd see a coil of it layin' behind a tree, that you never know'd was there, and layin' there lookin' like it was ready to spring at you. The teamsters met themselves comin' back so many times while drivin' over it, that it begun to get on their nerves and we come near havin' a crazy-house in camp there. And so Paul made up his mind that that there road was goin' to be straightened out right then and there, and he went after it accordin'.

What he done was, he went out and told Bill to bring up

BABE'D WALK RIGHT OFF WITH IT

the Blue Ox right away, and hitch him to the near end of the road.

Then he went up and spoke somethin' kind of low to Babe, and then afterwards he went out kind of to one side himself, and Babe laid hold, and then is the time it come pretty near breakin' the Ox in two, like I said.

"Come on, Babe! Co-ome on, Ba-abe!" says Paul, and the Ox lays hold and pulls to the last ounce of him. If I live to be a hundred years old I never hope to see an ox pull like that again. His hind legs laid straight out behind him nearly, and his belly was almost down touchin' the ground.

It was one beeg job, as the Frenchmen would of said. And when the crooks finally was all out of that there piece of road, there was enough of it to lay around a round lake we skidded logs into that winter, and then there was enough left in the place where it'd been at first to reach from one end to the other.

I've always been glad I saw Babe on that pull, for it's the greatest thing I ever saw him do—in its way, anyway.

Bill, that took care of the Blue Ox, generally went by the name of Brimstone Bill at camp and the reason was because he got to be so awfully red-hot tempered. But I never blamed him, though. Havin' that Ox to take care of was enough to make a sinner out of the best fellow that ever lived. Of all the scrapin' and haulin' you'd have to do to keep him lookin' anywheres near respectable even, no one would ever think.

And the way he ate—it took two men just to pick the balin' wire out of his teeth at mealtimes. Four ton of grain wasn't nothin' for Babe to get away with at a single meal, and for the hay—I can't mention quantities, but I know they

said at first, before he got Windy Knight onto cuttin' it up
for nails to use in puttin' on the cook-house roof, Paul used
to have to move the camp every two weeks to get away from
the mess of haywire that got collected where Babe ate his
dinner. And as for cleanin' the barn and haulin' the manure
away—

I remember one night in our bunkhouse as plain as if it'd
been yesterday. I can see it all again just like it was then. That
was one time afterwards, when we was loggin' down in Wisconsin.

There was a new fellow just come to camp that day, a kind
of college fellow that'd come to the woods for his health,
and we was all sittin' around the stove that night spinnin'
yarns like we almost always done of an evenin' while our socks
was dryin'. I was over on one end, and to each side of me was
Joe Stiles, and Pat O'Henry—it's funny how I remember
it all—and a fellow by the name of Horn, and Big Gus, and
a number of others that I don't recollect now, and over on
the other end opposite me was Brimstone Bill, and up by me
was this new fellow, but kind of a little to the side.

Well, quite a number of stories had been told, and some
of 'em had been about the Blue Ox and different experiences
men'd had with him different times and how the manure used
to pile up, and pretty soon that there college chap begun to
tell a story he said it reminded him of—one of them there
old ancient Greek stories, he said it was, about Herukles
cleanin' the Augaen stables, that was one of twelve other
hard jobs he'd been set to do by the king he was workin' for
at the time, to get his daughter or somethin' like that. He
was goin' at it kind of fancy, describin' how the stables hadn't

been cleaned for some time, and what a condition they was
in as a consequence, and what a strong man Herukles was,
and how he adopted the plan of turnin' the river right
through the stables and so washin' the manure away that way,
and goin' on describin' how it was all done. And how the
water come through and floated the manure all up on top
of the river, and how there was enough of it to spread over
a whole valley, and then how the manure rolled up in waves
again in the river when it got to where it was swifter—and
it was a pretty good story and he was quite a talker too, that
young fellow was, and he had all the men listenin' to him.

Well, all the time old Brimstone Bill he sat there takin'
it all in, and I could see by the way his jaw was workin' on
his tobacco that he was gettin' pretty riled. Everythin' had
been quiet while the young fellow was tellin' the story, and
some of us was smokin', some of us enjoyin' a little fresh
Star or Peerless maybe and spittin' in the sandbox occasionally
which was gettin' pretty wet by this time, and there wasn't
no sound at all except the occasional sizzle when somebody
hit the stove, or the movin' of a bench when somebody's foot
or sock would get too near the fire, and the man's voice goin'
along describin' about this Herukles and how great he was
and how fine the stables looked when he got through with
'em, when all at once Brimstone Bill he busted right into
him:

"You shut your blamed mouth about that Herik Lees of
yourn," he says. "I guess if your Herik Lees had had the
job I've got for a few days, he wouldn't of done it so easy
or talked so smart, you young Smart Alec, you—" and then
a long string of 'em the way Bill could roll 'em off when he

got mad—I never heard any much better'n him—they said he could keep goin' for a good half hour and never repeat the same word twict—but I wouldn't give much for a lumber-jack who couldn't roll off a few dozen straight—specially if he's worked with cattle—and all the time he was gettin' madder'n madder till he was fairly sizzlin' he was so mad. "I guess if that Mr. Lees had had Babe to take care of he wouldn't of done it so easy. Tell him he can trade jobs with me for a spell if he wants to, and see how he likes it. I guess if he'd of had to use his back on them one hundred and fifty jacks to jack up the barn the way I got to do he wouldn't of had enough strength left in him to brag so much about it. I just got through raisin' it another sixty foot this afternoon. When this job started we was workin' on the level, and now already Babe's barn is up sixteen hundred foot. I'd like to see the river that could wash that pile of manure away, and you can just tell that Herik Lees to come on and try it if he wants to. And if he can't, why, then you can just shut up about it. I've walked the old Ox and cleaned 'im and doctored 'im and rubbed 'im ever since he was first invented, and I know what it is, and I ain't goin' to sit here and let you tell me about any Mr. Lees or any other blankety blank liar that don't know what he's talkin' about tellin' about cleanin' barns— not if I know it." And at it he goes again blankety blank blank all the way out through the door, and slams it behind him so the whole bunkhouse shook, and the stranger he sits there and don't know hardly what to make of it. Till I kind of explained to him afterwards before we turned in, and we all, the rest of 'em too, told him not to mind about Bill, for he couldn't hardly help it. After he'd been in camp a few days

he'd know. You couldn't hardly blame Bill for bein' aggra-
vated—used to be a real good-natured man, and he wasn't
so bad even that time I was helpin' him, but the Ox was too
much for any man, no matter who.

And so I never held it against Bill much myself. He was
fond of Babe too and made quite a pet of him, more so than
the rest of us even, and we all did.

"I been with the beast a good long time," he used to say,
"and I know the cantankerous old reptile most the same's if
I had been through him with a lantern. I know how to do
for 'im, and all his little ways and all, and I don't want anybody else botherin' round and messin' things up for me. I can
take care of 'im all right. All I want is to be let alone."

Afterwards when Paul got his hay farm down in Wisconsin it made it easier for Bill. Then we'd just rake the hay
up in windrows and let it freeze that way layin' out across
the fields, and in the winter they'd haul it in one end first
in the stable and cut it up in chunks for Babe, just pullin' it
up a little each time. That way you could get away from the
nuisance of the haywire, and didn't have that to bother with.

In any of his small camps Paul couldn't never keep Babe
but a day or so at a time, because it took the tote-teamsters
a year to haul a day's feed for him.

Babe was a kind of playful fellow too. Sometimes he'd step
in a river and lay down there and so make the water rise and
leave a boom of logs that was below there up high and dry,
and again sometimes he'd step on a ridge makin' a lakeshore
maybe, and smash it down and let out the water to flood a
river and drown out some low water drive.

Around the camp he'd play with almost any of us who was

willin' to play with him after the day's work. We used to
feed him hotcakes sometimes and he got awful fond of 'em.
Them big ones we made on the big griddle we used to fold
up in quarters and put clover hay in between and give it to
him for a sandwich and he liked that powerful well. But
we shouldn't of done it, I know that now. I've thought many
times since, it's too bad, for that's what got him started, and
once started he seemed he couldn't never stop. Poor old Babe.
It proved to be the death of him at last. It was all wrong of
us, but of course we didn't think about it then, and had no
notion what it would lead to in the end.

Paul Bunyan was sure fond of his Ox, and mighty proud
of him too, as he'd a right to be.

"Be faithful," he used to say to him low under his breath
as he walked along beside him. "Be faithful, my Babe. Faithful."

THE ROUND DRIVE

AUL logged in Michigan
for about five years after that, and then we went up into Wisconsin, to a new part where we hadn't never been before.
One year, I know, up there, we was loggin' on a river that
we didn't even know the name of till we happened to find
out the next spring when we was pretty near ready to leave
anyway.

That spring Shot Gunderson, Joe Murphy, Pete Hackett,
and myself was goin' to take the drive down for Paul; and
then we had a number of others along too—they was most of
'em pretty good rivermen—and then for good luck we had
Pete Legoux along. I'll have to stop and tell about Pete some
time, for he sure was about as fool a Frenchman as you ever
want to see. One time I remember he made Paul pretty good
and mad at him.

Paul had a raft of logs in the river that he was goin' to
take down to the mill afterwards but that he wanted to tie
up for the time bein' till he could get another lot out first.
Well, the way it was, Paul himself was out on the boom
fastenin' up the boom chains, and the river was roarin' along
pretty fast right there, and he'd left Pete up at the other
end by the windlass with the anchor, and when he got the
boom in just the right location to suit him, he yells to Pete,
"Drop the anchor, Pete!"

And Pete he looks down at the anchor and he sees there
ain't no rope on it, and he yells back to Paul:

"Hey, Paul, no string on hank'."

But course with the roar of the river and all the noise it
made, Paul didn't hear, and he yells again, "Drop the anchor,
Pete. What's the matter with you? Drop the anchor, I said."

And then Pete he drops the anchor. "What Paul say, she
go," he says to himself. "Paul, he ees ze boss and he make all
ze monee from log. When he say, 'Drop ze hank',' I drop ze
hank'. By Gar! Eef Paul say drop ze horse, I drop ze horse."

And so the minute Paul let go, the boom went spinnin'
down the rapids, naturally, and the anchor was safe in the
mud at the bottom of the river, and Paul would of liked to've
fell in and got drowned if he hadn't of turned the log he was
on around and made it float up river so's he could get to land.
And he sure was mad at Pete that time.

But here now I've been tellin' all about Pete, when I was
goin' to tell about the Round Drive. And for that matter
that ain't all about Pete Legoux neither—I'll have to tell the
rest some other time, I guess.

Well, there was Shot Gunderson and Joe Murphy, and

Pete Hackett and myself and a number of others and we was goin' to take the drive down that spring. There'd been this river close to where we was loggin' and we'd been puttin' all the logs we got out that winter into this river we was on—about twenty-six million feet I reckon there must of been in all—and Paul told us to take 'em down to a mill somewheres and sell 'em.

Well, we didn't know where we was exactly, but we figgured if we followed the "usual plan and drove the way the river ran," like they say in the poetry, we'd come out somewheres, and so we started out.

Hackett was cookin' for the gang and Joe and me and Shot was takin' turns actin' as river-boss, and we was movin' along havin' a gay time, laughin' and talkin' and singin', and that's the way we went on down the river for about two weeks or three pretty near, and nothin' happened all that time, and then what did we do one day but run by a camp that looked pretty near as big as ours, and we wondered who it was that was loggin' there, naturally.

But of course we didn't stop to investigate, because we didn't think so very much about it then, but kept right on goin'.

And then pretty soon, after about another two or three weeks or so, we passed another camp that looked even bigger than the first one had done. There was the same cook-house pretty near like in our own camp, with the stove-pipe and the smoke comin' out of it, and there was the barns for the cattle and the manure piles and everythin', and the stacks of wood that the bull-cooks had got in, behind the cook-shanty, and the blacksmith shop and all, and all just exactly like we had in our camp—only not quite so big, of course, but pretty near—and we wondered who it was that was loggin' on anythin' like that scale, almost like Paul, and was apin' his methods like that, and we talked about it almost every day after that for the next couple of weeks. And then I'll be jiggered if we didn't run into another camp again, just the same as the other two that we'd passed before.

So that time we thought we'd stop and investigate, and we did.

"I'm goin' to go ashore," I says. "I don't care what the rest of you is goin' to do."

And Shot Gunderson, he says, "I'm with you, Angus. Just wait a minute. I'll go up with you."

And the two of us went up towards the camp.

"If we find out who the fellow is, runnin' this outfit," says Shot, "we'll just tell him Paul's got all the land in this part of the state pre-empted, and he'd better be thinkin' about movin' out if he knows what's good for him.

"And Paul's got a patent on them there kind of skid sleds," he says, "and this feller'd better not be usin' 'em, or he'll find out."

"Looks like he's got a blue ox to log with too," I says. "Look at that barn up there." For there was a big barn just like Babe's up on the hill.

"Paul will sure be mad when he finds out about this," Shot says.

And by that time we was pretty near up to the commissary, and we was all ready with what we was goin' to say to that boss when we found him, and here if we didn't run right plank, slam into Paul himself as big as you please, sittin' on the commissary steps in the sunshine whittlin' on a jackpine. By George, we was some surprised.

You see the way that was, the river we'd been on was round and hadn't no outlet, and we'd been goin' round and round the same way all them eight weeks we'd been out, and them three camps we'd passed had been nothin' but our own camp all the time.

"Ef we go roun' an' roun' some more, las' we go to hal," says Pete Legoux. And I guess that time Pete would of been about right.

And so then, when the drive came back that way, Paul finally knowed where he'd been loggin' that winter.

"We been loggin' on Round River," he says. "I kind of pretty near thought that from what happened the other day."

What'd happened the other day was:

Sam's supply of meat was gettin' low and Paul knowed there must be some good fish in that river and he figgured he'd go out and get a supply of 'em to help out with.

So he got Ole to make him a water auger, and then, like he generally did, he went out and bored holes. That's the way Paul almost always done his fishin'. He'd bore holes in the river and then when the fish would come to these holes they'd fall down in 'em and break their necks. Dead fish always float, of course, and Paul'd get the cook's coffee-strainer and use that for a landin'-net.

But there was something funny about them fish, though. They was curved, and Ole had to make all extra round bottoms for the frying-pans for the cook to fry 'em in. And then when the men ate 'em it made their backs get all crooked up so Paul had to put quite a few of 'em in splints to get them straightened out again.

So Paul was pretty near beginning to think that there was something queer about that river, and now when we told him the luck we'd had he knowed where he was all right.

"It's Round River we been loggin' on," he says. "No wonder them fish was kind of funny."

And so that was the end of the Round Drive. Well, that is, of course, we had to get the logs out, but Paul fixed that up all right. What he done was, he just called Sourdough Sam, the cook.

"Sam," he says, "make up a good stiff batch of sourdough biscuit dough, and when I get ready, you put it in where I tell you to."

And then he goes out right away and spades out a channel through a ridge that's between the river and a lake over on the other side, that's got an outlet. And next mornin' Sam dumps his sourdough in the big tank and hitches Babe to it and hauls it out and dumps it in the river, and it riz right up and filled the channel and floated the logs right out into the lake. And so then Shot and I and Joe and the rest of the men started out again, gay as ever.

The spring drive, of course, used to always be a great time for us lumberjacks. It was a mighty excitin' time, and then besides it was a pretty sight too. Floatin' down one of them rivers on fine balmy spring nights, I tell you it was fine.

The willows would be hangin' down to the water on each side, swishin' as we went by, and the pine trees up on the hills would be black as pitch against the sky. Oh, it used to be a fine sight—would make a mighty fine picture, I've

always thought. And the water lappin' against the sides of
the raft we was on, and against the old rotten logs layin' out
along the banks of the stream. Talk about your fine music.
If that wasn't fine music for you, I'd like to know. And

sometimes you'd be passin' through them cool layers of air
that made you shiver and turn up your mackinaw around
your neck, and then again sometimes you'd hit one of them
warm layers that's so soft and warm on your face that it near
puts you to sleep and you feel as if you'd never want to wake
up no more. Funny how I remember it all, how it used to be
on them Wisconsin rivers in the spring. I don't suppose I'd
thought of it for maybe forty years.

I never did rightly understand what caused them warm
layers and them cool layers of air like that. I've noticed 'em
in other places too. Down on the farm where I was a boy,
along the cricks down there. It's always puzzled me, and
though I've heard it talked about a good deal, I never yet
met anybody that knowed what made 'em that way.

Yes, and then always there was the white-water drivin'.
That used to be a pretty sight too. And Paul was the greatest
white-water man that ever was.

There wasn't nobody could shoot a falls or a rapids like
him—or anywheres near like him except one man; and that
was the fellow the St. Lawrence River was named after. It
was when Paul was bringin' a raft of logs around Key West
from his South Dakota camps to take 'em up to Chicago and
he was on the lookout for some place to take 'em through.

Well, he found a river and started up it, but pretty soon
he come to the Niagara Falls and he didn't know how he
was goin' to make the climb.

"Gee, I guess I've got to have some help," he says.

And then he went up to a farmer's that lived on the banks
of the stream, and as luck would have it he was a regular
old seasoned French-Canadian white-water man, the best of

any, and between the two of 'em they got the raft over the falls all right. The man's name was Lawrence, so Paul Bunyan named the crick the Saint Lawrence in honor of him.

Well, drivin' was a fine excitin' time like I said, most ways —course there was some drawbacks—the mosquitoes, for instance. They was as big as grasshoppers, and no mistake. They said some of 'em used to lay in hollow logs and bark at night, but it seems to me most of 'em was out that time of day.

Paul tried a cure for the mosquitoes once but that's one of the times he didn't do so good as he thought he was goin' to.

He sent East somewhere for a few hives of a special big kind of bumblebees, and he figgured it out that the bumblebees would eat the mosquitoes so we'd get rid of 'em, and then the bumblebees that was left wouldn't bother us none if we'd only leave 'em alone—and they might make honey on the side. Well, what happened was, the bumblebees, instead of bein' mortal enemies of the mosquitoes as they should of been, made friends with 'em instead and got so thick with 'em that the two tribes intermarried. The youngsters was some terrors, let me tell you. They had the big fat body of their bumblebee dads and the longishness and leanness of their mosquito mothers, and a sting they come by from each of 'em, so they had a stinger in each end of 'em. That way they got us both goin' and comin'.

Well, it was an awful life we led after that. We used to have to barricade the doors and windows of the stables so that the things wouldn't get at the cattle, and we had men with axes, and peavies, and pike-poles standin' guard on the inside. They got so hungry they tore the shakes off the bunkhouse roof tryin' to get in, and they come pretty near carryin' off the whole camp.

Finally, though, the bumblebee blood in 'em got the best of 'em. Terrible fond of sweets they was, like their dads, only more so, and they couldn't never get enough. Course there was flowers growin' round the camp, but what's a flower to a bee with a ten gallon stomach?

And one day they smelled a sugar ship out in the middle of Lake Superior comin' from Hawaii, carryin' a carload of sugar to Paul's camp, and they all swarmed out to get some. They killed off all the crew and got the sugar all right, but they got more'n was good for 'em. They was so greedy and ate till they got so heavy that when they tried to fly back to shore, they sunk in the lake and was never heard of no more.

Only a few of 'em was left and them P. T. Barnum got for his circus. Mr. Barnum had wanted Babe if he could of got him, but Paul said he couldn't afford to let him go, and he wouldn't think of it anyway, but he told old P. T. if he wanted some of them there mosquitoes, why, he was welcome to 'em.

Well, when Barnum heard about them mosquitoes and what a size they was and some of the things they could do, he was just as crazy to get them as he'd been about gettin' Babe—anyway he couldn't of found tunnels big enough to take the Ox through with his circus train but would of had to have special men to turn Babe's head sideways every time they was goin' to go through one—and so then right away he sends up one of his best lion-tamers to capture a few of them mosquitoes.

That feller that come up—Henderlee, his name was—was

IT WAS AN AWFUL LIFE WE LED AFTER THAT

sure a game young feller all right. First thing one of them mosquitoes pretty near killed him—tore a good part of his shirt off of him first thing and got a big hunk out of his shoulder, just above the left shoulder-blade when he was tryin' to get a half-Nelson on him.

He might of tried the boiler method of catchin' 'em, but someone told him that wasn't no good. Don Howard had tried that way of doin' it but found it didn't work very good —Don was that young college chap we had in camp, and he was goin' to get some of them mosquitoes to take back to one of his perfessors, he said. Well, he got himself a good heavy copper boiler and crawled under that, and used himself as bait, and took a good big hammer in with him, and he figgured when the mosquitoes would stick their snouts in he'd just hammer 'em down and rivet 'em fast to the inside of the boiler. But he hadn't riveted no more'n three of them till they got so strong they just flew away, boiler and all, liftin' it right up with 'em.

Well, one of the men at the camp told Barnum's man about that, so he had sense enough not to try that way.

"I know what I'll do," he says. "I'll catch 'em all right. I got a way, I think."

And what he done was, he got a squirt gun and shot turpentine up at 'em, and when it landed on their stomachs where the hair was thin it hurt 'em and they doubled up with pain. Their stingers was made with a kind of crook at the end and when they got curled up like that they got their hind stinger caught around their front stinger and got held up tight in a ring. So then Henderlee clamped a chain on quick and a padlock and loaded 'em in cars in rings that way and shipped 'em down to Chicago, where the circus was at the time.

But he was a game feller all right. For if he hadn't of had good luck the turpentine might of made 'em so mad that they would of killed him right off without stoppin' to sing a warnin'. It was good figgurin' on his part to know they'd catch themselves around the stingers that way.

And that same spring of the mosquitoes was the time the bedbugs got so thick in camp too. We'd been so busy fightin' the mosquitoes that we'd kind of let up on the bedbugs for a spell and they'd got the run on us. They got so smart that when you wrote your name down in the big time-book in the office and the clerk put down the number of the bunk you was goin' to sleep in, the bedbugs would crawl along the pen so's to know where to find you afterwards.

And they always found you, too.

PRUNESTONES

N PAUL'S camp back there in Wisconsin the prunestones used to get so thick they had to have twenty ox-teams haulin' 'em away, and they hauled 'em out in the woods, and the chipmunks ate 'em and grew so big the people shot 'em for tigers.

The big scale everythin' was, of course, like I've been tellin' about, you couldn't hardly help it. Bound to be a mess. Paul used to have twenty flunkies sweepin' the prunestones out from under the tables, but even then they'd get so thick we had to wade through 'em up over our shoes sometimes on our way in to dinner. They'd be all over the floor and in behind the stove and piled up against the windows where they'd dumped 'em outside so the cook couldn't see out at all hardly.

We begun to have so many Swedes in camp there always,

and of course that was the reason. And Paul just had to have
the prunes for 'em if he was goin' to get any work out of
'em at all—prunes and snoos. Paul took to chewin' snoos himself one winter and it kept two men busy shovelin' for him
all the time.

But generally, though, Paul was satisfied with smokin' a
pipe—one of them there big corn-cobs, he used to have—
strong enough to buck a northeast wind. He lost it one time
and didn't find it for pretty near a week and then he got so
grumpy nobody couldn't hardly get along with him. But one
of the bull-cooks made him up a kind of cigar out of some
of the patent tar roofing they was puttin' on the cook-shanty
roof at the time and filled it up inside with some of the coffee
grounds the cook had on hand, and that was strong enough
to put Paul in good humor again till his pipe could be found
and hauled back to camp.

And the eggshells, too, used to be thick—so deep we generally had to dig a runway through to get in the cook-house
door. But even at their worst they wasn't anywhere near as
bad as the prunestones of course. Paul raked up eighteen carloads of the prunestones one winter and shipped 'em out and
Charley Dobey told me he got $40,000 for 'em. I always
wondered what anybody'd be wantin' to buy prunestones for
but afterwards I found out. It seems some Foreign Trade Ex-
portin' Company was shippin' 'em to South America, riveted
together in long strings, to sell 'em to the natives for wenie-
wursts.

And another winter when he had some extra big prunes
from California, Paul used a lot of 'em to build a prune-
stone bridge across Lake Superior.

Paul was loggin' on the south shore of the lake that winter near Ashland and had his camp on the north shore. The lake was frozen over pretty well, but there was about five miles right in the middle that wasn't froze over, and so Paul didn't have no way of gettin' the crew across to Wisconsin to work unless he built a bridge. He started in to build it just over the open place at first, just lettin' it come out even at the end, but then he figgured he might as well have it extend over on the ice a little ways too while he was at it so the slope would be better, and anyway he had plenty of prune-stones to work with and plenty of haywire. He used haywire to bale 'em up with. He'd bale the prunestones together with wire and then he'd raise the bales up on end and you'd find they wasn't such poor material for a bridge neither when you got a few of 'em put together.

It came in mighty handy afterwards when Paul started his macaroni farm down in Wisconsin. That bridge was 14,000 feet long, 4,000 feet high on each side, and 4 feet wide, and was built far enough out over the ice so it held good for many years afterwards.

And then, besides prunes, another thing we had in camp there always was pea-soup—that's when there was French-men around and that was pretty generally all the time, for Paul was awfully fond of the Frenchmen for loggers.

"Nothing like the Frenchmen for loggers," he used to say, "when they have their pea-soup." And he generally seen to it that they had it.

Breakfast, pea-soup, dinner, pea-soup, supper, pea-soup, it didn't make no difference, the Frenchmen was always just as fond of it.

We used to have a big dinnerhorn in camp that the cook'd send one of the cookees out to blow, whenever dinner was ready, and the minute them Frenchmen heard that horn begin to toot they'd make a bee-line right off for the cook-shack.

No matter where they was or what they was doin' they'd be off right away and in a minute or two they'd be settin' down eatin' their pea-soup. If they was out in the woods and choppin' down a tree, even if their ax was up in the air on the stroke they was makin', they wouldn't bother to finish it but would leave it up there in the air and break for the camp.

"Come on, boys, good pea-soup on ze tab," one of 'em would yell, and they'd all go helter-skelter, hit-er-miss, as fast as they could leg it.

I remember there was a buyer come out from New York once and he was out in the woods with some of the men tryin' to get a line-up on the way loggin' was done and how the logs was first got out that his lumber come from so's he'd know somethin' about it from the beginnin'. Well, he'd been watchin' the fallers and the buckers and the way the loadin' was done, spendin' most of the forenoon, and he happened to be out there by the road when the dinnerhorn blowed, and he was sure surprised at the way the men come out of the woods on both sides down the slopes of the hill. I guess he thought the woods was a-fire or some terrible animal was after 'em, for here they come, runnin' like mad, as hard as they could go.

They all run past him, of course, and it wasn't long, runnin' the way they did, till they was all gone by. All but one, that is. The buyer noticed this fellow wasn't runnin' no more. It seems he'd been knocked down by somebody, and when he got up again he didn't try to run no more but just walked along slow.

"Why ain't you runnin'?" Smith says to him. "You ain't hurt, are you? You ought to be runnin' like the rest of 'em."

"No use run no more," Frenchie says. "Pee-soup all gone now when I come."

You had to be right there always if you was goin' to get any of the pea-soup, for it seems the cook couldn't never make enough to fill up all them Frenchmen, but they always had room for more.

That was before we had the pea-soup spring, of course, while they was just cookin' it in kettles. After we got the pea-soup spring it was all right.

The way Paul happened to get the spring was: One afternoon one of the tote-teamsters was comin' along the road from town with a load of peas for the camp. It was in March and the road was gettin' slippery, and there was a hot spring alongside the road and the steam from there made it all the more slippery right in that spot, and just as the teamster was comin' by that slippery place the sled begun to slide off the ice-road and the whole tote-load went right kerplunk into the spring, load, teamster, cattle and all—that is, the young teamster managed to keep himself out and most part of the cattle—their hind legs was in, that was all—but the load of peas went clean to the bottom, and naturally the young feller didn't know what to do.

Well, about that time Paul come along and the minute he seen how it was he knowed what to do, for Paul wasn't never stumped, and this give him one of his bright ideas again.

"Unyoke the cattle," he says to the teamster, "and get

out of the way yourself. And hand me that ax and peavey you got there."

And then he takes and butchers the cattle and cuts the meat up in hunks and pushes the whole outfit back in the spring again.

"Let it cook a couple of hours," he says, "and then you can tell the men to come up for their pea-soup. It'll be fine, flavored with oxtail that way."

Most loggin' bosses if they'd of lost a load that way would of considered it an entire total loss but that wasn't Paul. Paul always knowed what to do in a case like that.

And so after that we always cooked the pea-soup in that spring. Paul had a splash dam and flume put in after a while so he could run a soup splash down to the camps on section 37, and out to the men that was workin' too far out in the woods to come in at dinner time.

Paul used to have the peas shipped in by the trainload and the same way with the salt pork and beef, and flour for the hotcakes. The prune trains always came in with two engines on 'em, one before, and one behind, pushing.

We had spuds in Paul's camp, too. We didn't use to at first, but the men liked 'em with their salt pork and so Paul thought he'd get a supply of 'em. But one spring someone left the warehouse door open and the sun came in on the sacks of potatoes and turned 'em all green and spoiled 'em all for eatin'. Paul was mad, and he said he was goin' to raise some himself.

"I'm goin' to have new potatoes by the Fourth of July," he says.

Course most of us told him it couldn't be done, but Paul

HE COULD JUST REACH UP AND GET ONE

said he'd show us, and so he went ahead and grubbed up a
south slope a little ways from the camp and put in his spuds.

Well, it was a fine spring with plenty of sunshine, and the
vines was growin' fine and big, and about the first of July
Paul went out to see if his bet was goin' to be good or not.

He went about a quarter of the way up the hill and made
a little hole by one of the vines, workin' pretty carefully, and
it's a good thing he did go about it carefully or it might have
been worse, for thirty-seven bushel run out of that there hole
before he could get it plugged up again.

And so we had plenty of spuds that next winter, and afterwards that's the way Paul always done—just planted 'em
himself.

Then besides the prunestones and eggshells and potato
peelin's there was the coffee grounds that always got collected around the cook-shanty door and had to be hauled
away. Till towards spring anyhow, when we could let 'em
pile up then for a time because we was goin' to move camp
soon anyway. One of the cookees was goin' to try to get away
from the coffee grounds by not puttin' any coffee in, but just
drawin' his brown shirt through the coffee-pot instead, but
the men wouldn't stand for that. Just the same as they
wouldn't stand for the religious cook neither.

Paul hired an awful religious cook that spring by the name
of Heaven-Help-Us Davis, that was bound that grace was
goin' to be said at the table at meal time. Naturally the men
wouldn't stand for it—didn't want several minutes of perfectly good eatin' time wasted in askin' grace. So Paul didn't
know what to do about the men kickin', because good cooks
was awful hard to find, and Heaven-Help-Us was a mighty

good cook, even if he did mix revival hymns in with the onions in the mulligan like they said he did—it don't cut much ice what goes into a mulligan anyway.

Well, it looked for a while as if there was goin' to be a real row in camp, because the men was all rarin' mad, and Heaven-Help-Us wouldn't give in on a little grace at meals anyway, and then Paul he thought of somethin'. What he done was, he hired a tall, lank guy for a cookee to help wait on table and so they didn't have to ask no grace no more after that. That feller was so blame tall he could just reach up and get one without havin' to ask for it.

Now how wide did I put that bridge down for? What was it I said, I wonder. Oh, four feet. No, that ain't right. Four feet ain't wide enough for a bridge. I thought there was something wrong there. It was 40,000 feet long, 14,000 feet high, and 40 feet wide—forty, that's what it was. Them was the exact measurements that was give to me by the engineer that was puttin' it up.

Funny thing when you get something like that wrong, how it bothers you afterwards, till you just got to go back and fix it up. It might not bother some people, but I always want to get everything right if I can. The truth, the whole truth and nothing but the truth, is the way I want it should be.

ESIDES Paul himself
bein' great he had some men workin' for him that was A-1
too. I can't say I ever got to be so much around the camp myself—I wasn't the size to be a great logger like some of 'em
was—but there was some, all right, that Paul was mighty
proud of. Course I was six foot two or three in them days—
when I was young, that is—and that ain't so bad—I've sunk
down a good bit since then—you kind of settle down when
you get old, you'll find—but that wasn't nothin' to compare
with some of 'em—Ole, f'rinstance, that I've mentioned, and
Batiste Joe, and Windy and Shot and the rest of them. Oh,
Paul and I always got along all right when it comes to that
and I guess he liked me all right, but he wasn't fond of me
like he was of Ole, and Joe, and them others.

There was a funny thing about Ole when he first come to

camp—Paul come near makin' a bad mistake about him. You
see it was like this: Paul'd been needin' a cook and a blacksmith both for a long time, and he'd been advertisin' for 'em;
and one mornin' two men comes up to the camp lookin' for
a job, and the ticket says one of 'em is a cook and the other
is a blacksmith. Well, Paul was mighty glad to get 'em and
right away he says to the one with the clean shirt on:

"You get right into that cook-shanty and start the hotcakes. You're just the man I been lookin' for."

And to the other fellow—the one with the dirty shirt—
he says:

"My Ox needs a shoe on his left hind foot. The blacksmith shop is over there. You'll find a carload of iron in."

And then, naturally, he goes away and leaves 'em, for Paul
wasn't the kind that waited for an answer to the orders he
give. And they just had to make the best of it.

But it wasn't long before Paul found out the mistake he'd
made, though, and the rest of us found out too when we come
in to breakfast, for Ole tempered the hotcakes so hard they
was just like iron. And the cook, that was tryin' to be the
blacksmith, started to soak off Babe's hoof with hot oatmeal
mush instead of parin' it off, and pretty near got his head
kicked off in the bargain.

Well, when Paul took the first bite into one of them hotcakes, he seen what he'd done soon enough, and was pretty
prompt to make it right.

"Go out there," he says to Ole, "and make a left hind shoe
for that Blue Ox of mine. If you get the iron anywheres
near as hard as this hotcake, it'll wear on any ice-road we got,
I reckon. And tell that partner of yours out there to come in

and make breakfast for the camp."

And so Ole the Blacksmith got his right job all right, and the cook got his. But I tell you Ole was mighty careful never to wear a clean shirt again—never after that, not even when he was courtin'. That breakfast was all he wanted of it. All he ever had to do with the cookin' after that was to punch the holes in the doughnuts for Paul—that was a big job, of course, but then that come naturally in his line.

But Slim Mullins didn't never change his shirt—that would of been too much for him, I spose. He'd got so used to the one he had on, that he couldn't never seem to think of changin' it. At least I never knowed of it if he did. So long as I knowed him he always wore that same shirt.

Of course it never wore out, naturally, for he always kept gettin' a new layer of grease on it all the time, and that kept it from wearin' out. It got so slippery at last that they said he used to have to sleep between sandpapers to keep from slippin' out of bed. He went away with it on when Johnny Inkslinger had to mix him up a walk at last, because he'd put dynamite in the biscuits instead of bakin' powder when he was drunk one day, and if that cook is around somewhere now I'll bet my last dollar he's wearin' that shirt yet.

And another feller that come into camp about the same time and afterwards got to be one of the best men there was Bud Kangley. He was a green kid when he first come in and we used to like to play tricks on him. A big strappin' youngster just off the farm, with blue eyes and yellow hair and pink cheeks—just the kind you like to play a good joke on—with big muscles, though soft yet of course, but the makin's of a first-rate logger in him.

Well, we all liked to get somethin' on Bud, he always
was so good-natured and used to get such a fine big grin on
when he found out he'd been fooled, but one time one of the
straw bosses—a kind of smart-Alec, Red Hawley—went a
little too far, though. He sent Bud to Ashland over forty
miles away to get a crosshaul, and the kid didn't know no
better than to start out to go after it.

But he caught on, I guess, pretty soon after he got into
town, and so what he done was, he just kept on lookin' for
that crosshaul all winter. And in the spring he got a lawyer
and the two of 'em come out to camp and presented Hawley
with a bill for Bud's expenses in town that winter and his
wages, and some entertainment thrown in, and the cost of
legal services and advice, and Red had to foot the bill. He'd
sent Bud to town to look for a crosshaul and that's what Bud
had been doin', and so he didn't have no comeback, but had
to pay it out of his own pocket. Red didn't stick around very
long after that but went off somewhere else to another camp,
I guess. And Kangley got to be one of the best men in camp,
just about as good at anything he'd turn his hand to, and big
and strong like an ox, and equal to about six ordinary loggers.

And then, Shot Gunderson I mentioned before; he was a
good friend of mine, but pretty near too fond of hunting for
a real logger—though he was pretty steady, too. I know one
time when we was loggin' up there he went out and caught a
bear one Sunday and brought him home and trained him for
a saddle bear. In the fall there for a couple of months, before
the cold weather set in, he could have pretty good sport with
him. But one time he went out huntin' bear with some of the
other fellows from camp and he was ridin' this saddle bear—

MUST OF IN THE FIGHT GOT MIXED UP SOMEWAY

Molar is what he had named him—and that time the fight got to be pretty fast and furious, I guess. Anyway Shot lost his gun and had to get off and find it, and when he got back up on Molar's back he noticed he wasn't so gentle as he always generally was, and Shot didn't know what had got into him. But he toned down after a while, and Shot killed several of the other bear, and it wasn't till the huntin' party got home and Shot went to put Molar up for the night that he noticed it wasn't Molar at all but one of them wild bears that he'd rode home.

Must of in the fight got mixed up someway; and Molar must of been mistaken for a wild bear and been killed. I know Shot felt pretty blue for a while.

Of course that's where Shot Gunderson got his name from, that he was such a good shot and such a fine hunter. I don't believe I ever knew what his right name really was.

And then besides Shot Gunderson and Kangley, there was Charley Dobey, and Red Jack, and Blue-Nose Parker, and Batiste Joe, and a number of others that was about as good loggers as you'd ever want to find.

Batiste Joe was a Frenchman Paul'd had workin' for him ever since he was loggin' down around Lake Houghton and into the Muskegon River.

Joe generally took care of takin' the logs out for Paul, and done the scalin', and he was the best river-boss Paul ever had.

He was good, all right. The inspectors and buyers couldn't get ahead of him. I always wished I'd had a head on me like that fellow had. When he was there Paul didn't have to worry but what he'd get the best end of the deal all right.

Course the equipment Paul had was A-1—Joe couldn't of done much without good equipment. Like when it come to scalin' logs, f'rinstance. If they was too short, Joe just hitched the Blue Ox on 'em and pulled 'em out longer, and if they was too small through at the same time, he just had Babe pull out the butt end a little, and that made 'em bigger at the same time as makin' 'em longer, naturally. But Joe couldn't of done that without extra good equipment.

One time Paul had a drive on that he was sendin' down to Bay City. Batiste Joe was river-boss that spring, and on the way down he was arrested on a false charge of havin' stolen logs in his raft. Well, they took him into a court and the judge and lawyers started in on him, the way they do. But don't you believe them lawyer sharks could put anything over on Joe. All he knowed was they was Paul's logs. You might as well try to budge one of the Rocky Mountains as get Joe rattled; he'd been drivin' the white-water too long to let their noise bother him any.

"They is all Paul Bunyan log," says Joe. "I know 'em by ze mark."

"What mark?" roars one of the lawyers. "We didn't see no mark on 'em. That's just what's the trouble. They ain't got no mark—a lot of 'em hasn't."

"All ze time I know Paul Bunyan log," says Joe. "For all ze log with ze bark on they is Paul's—"

"And what about the ones with the bark off?" yells the lawyer, pickin' him up quick. "What about them, then?"

"All ze log with ze bark off," says Joe, "all ze log with ze bark off, they is Paul's too—I have all Paul Bunyan log in my boom."

So then of course they had to let him go, and he went on down and sold the logs for Paul.

Oh, some of the Frenchmen's smart all right. Joe sure had a good head on him. He wasn't like the other one we had, that Pete Legoux. I told about how he dropped the anchor for Paul once in the bottom of the lake, I guess, and I sure don't know why Paul didn't give him the sack the first day. I guess maybe he thought the men would have some fun with Pete. They had to have some fun in camp, and Paul maybe didn't care, one more or less on the payroll and to feed wouldn't make much difference.

But Pete thought he was some guy all right.

"Paul he should let me drive ze log," he says. "Paul he wer' queer guy. He say, 'Drop ze hank'!' and I drop ze hank', and then, by Gar, he get mad. Paul Bunyan ought to let me drive ze log, yah? Nobody good reever man like me. I can run on log and jump on log—fast. Like leetle animal wi' tail over hees head—wha' you call leetle animal wi' tail over hees head—run up tree so fast?"

"Cow," says Charley Nordstrom. "That's what you're thinkin' of, Pete, I guess."

"Oh, yah, cow. Cow is what I'm like. Pete Legoux he just like ze cow on ze log. So fast he can run."

Charley Dobey was the one that was generally left in charge when Paul had to go in town for a few days or go down on the ranch or go and contract for grub or somethin' like that. I guess he knowed more about Paul's business than anyone else around there. Charley and I was mighty good friends all the time we was in camp together.

One reason Paul liked him so well, I know, was because

of the way he could fiddle. Charley was a fine fiddler. He'd
sit there in the bunkhouse all evenin' sometimes and fiddle
away, and it was mighty fine to listen to the way he'd keep
time with his foot all the time. Them old tunes used to sound
mighty nice, and then sometimes Windy would sing some of
'em, and we'd all join in. If Charley happened to get on a
loose puncheon in the floor so the noise he made with his foot
would be almost as loud as the fiddlin' and the singin', we
wouldn't any of us think of quittin' till the straw boss would
come in and blow out the lights. Paul used to think Charley
was just about right—because he knowed if he could keep
the men contented that way, loggin' would go much better
and he wouldn't ever have no trouble keepin' his crews. I
didn't never understand why Paul didn't try to get Charley
for a son-in-law instead of Ole. But then of course Charley
wasn't the size Ole was.

Ole the Blacksmith was the only man in camp that could
swallow one of Sourdough Sam's soda biscuits whole, and
most generally he could do it in one bite, though sometimes
he'd have to take two or three. He always ate thirty-seven
eggs for breakfast, and a stack of hotcakes four foot high,
and bacon that was the lee side of a hog weighin' six hundred
pounds, and generally four pails full of coffee. He was the
nearest to Paul's size of any of the men, though then he
didn't come near bein' as tall as Paul by about two and a
half axhandles and wasn't anywheres near as strong or as
quick, of course. But I reckon, at that, Ole was the best man
Paul had, all right.

PAUL BUNYAN'S WIFE

WAS in camp two or three years before I ever knowed Paul had a wife but there was a Mrs. Paul all right, though I never got to know her so very well, for she didn't use to come out to camp so very often after I went to work for Paul. But I guess before that, when she was young, she used to come out real often. But after she got along a little older she stayed at home pretty close and worked on the farm, I guess.

Blue-Nose Parker told me one day how somebody was tellin' him how Paul first got hold of her.

It happened when Paul had a small camp on the Coulonge, one of his first, I guess. Him and one of the men was out gradin' a new road they was puttin' in when they heard a lot of hollerin' down by the Big Rapids.

"Sounds like a woman," Paul says. "That's too loud for

wildcats. We better see if we can help her."

And they both of 'em run over as fast as they could, and there was Carrie McIntie runnin' up and down the bank and callin' for help so you could hear her for ten miles away and her sister was just goin' over the falls and strugglin' manfully to get out, but it wasn't no use. Paul he didn't lose no time, he'd held onto his shovel and quick as a wink he started throwin' in dirt just above the girl and when Carrie seen his idea she pitched in and quit hollerin' and began throwin' in logs and rocks and anything she could get hold of and before you could say Jack Robinson they had a dam there that held the water back so's the girl could wade ashore on dry land.

You didn't have to hit Paul on the head with a sledge-hammer to make him see how quick Carrie was to get his idea, and the way she could handle them rocks and logs he knowed she'd make the right kind of a wife for a logger. And she'd be big enough too, he figgured, when she got her growth, for she was young yet. And so he up and asked her right there.

Carrie came over to the other side of the river, where Paul was, and after she kicked the dam out so the boom of logs down below wouldn't go aground, she said, "Sure"; and so they were married. And that's how Paul got his wife.

And she was of about a size to match himself when she finally got growed up. It took thirteen Hudson's Bay blankets to make her a skirt, and the sail of a full-rigged ship to make a waist for her.

And for shoes she'd just step into an extra big moose hide with each foot and then the shoemaker would sew it up round her ankle. He used to have to set down his box of tools six

times on the way round, markin' with chalk each time, so
he could know where to begin again after dinner.

When Paul had his macaroni farm down in Wisconsin, his
wife split most of the rails for fencin' it in.

But she kicked about that, though. She wasn't no ox, she
said, and so she wasn't goin' to split the rails for that farm—
not the whole lot of 'em anyway—and she made Paul hire
three French-Canadians to help her.

The Canadians contracted to split 900 rails a day, but Mrs.
Paul workin' alongside of 'em, split 4756 the first day they
went to work.

She was goin' pretty fast and they couldn't keep her in
sight at all, but the last rail she split, her ax stuck in a
splinter and she had to call on one of the Canucks to come
and get it out for her.

Well, he worked away for a while and finally he got it
out all right, but then he noticed there wasn't no head on the
ax—only the handle—and he went to look for it and he found
it in the first rail she'd split that mornin', so here she'd been
splittin' all day without no head on her ax.

And she could run too. She kept chickens and cows on the
farm and she had a dog, Quick, that she used to sic after the
cattle, before Teeny got big enough so she'd always fetch
'em for her.

Quick was a good dog and deserved his name all right, but
he wasn't so quick but what Mrs. Paul would always be
ahead of him and show him how to run when he was running
after the cattle.

"Come, Quick! Come, Quick!" she'd holler and she'd run
before him through the meadows and across the ditches and

alongside the brush-tracts and that way he'd bring the cows in for her night and morning.

She must of been pretty hot-tempered too, when she was young. She'd come out to camp sometimes and she'd flirt with the men and then she'd get mad at 'em and throw 'em around.

One time she was kind of sweet on one of the cooks Paul had, a man by the name of Chambers, and then I don't know what happened, he kind of quit bein' sweet on her, and she got mad and went in there one evenin' behind the stove where he was workin', and she give it to him, I can tell you.

And then after a little when she got tired and let up a bit he thought he'd try kindness on her and see what effect gentle words would have on her, and so he said:

"You know, I've been thinkin', dearie—"

And then I tell you she did get mad. There was a frypan of potatoes standin' there on the stove and she grabbed that up and went after him with it and give him a swipe over the head so the potatoes rained around him like a Nebraska hailstorm.

"Don't you dare 'dearie' me," she yells.

And then she give him a few more, and pretty soon the bottom had flew out of the frypan and only the rim was hangin' round his neck with the handle of it hangin' down in front.

"There!" she says, "now you've got a standup collar and a necktie too, and now are you satisfied, you lyin' deceiver you?" And with that she stalked away and left him.

But I guess after that she kind of lost the taste for flirtin' with the men, and didn't use to come around the camp so much no more. And she was gettin' older and got steadied down a good bit too, I guess. But she used to come out some-times, and we was generally glad to see her, and Paul always treated her real nice.

I know one time when I was workin' for Paul up there in Wisconsin she and some lady friends of hers come out to visit the camp, and they had dinner with the men in the cook-shack and seemed to have a real good time, lookin' around at things and watchin' the men work, and sittin' around sewin' part of the time, and they stayed most of the afternoon. And then just when they was gettin' ready to start for home a storm come up and it started in to rain, although it had been nice the whole afternoon before.

They had come down on a flatcar on the loggin' train and they was all goin' to get soakin' wet, but Paul knowed what to do. He uncoupled the engine from the train and hitched Babe onto the flatcar and started him down the track on a good brisk walk, and naturally they went so fast they missed every raindrop and didn't get wet at all, and so got home dry shod.

"No sense to lettin' the ladies get their feet wet," Paul says, "when we can fix it that easy."

And Mrs. Paul had a set of false teeth, I remember, that she was all-fired proud of, and then she was mighty fond of chicken too. Down on the farm she could have all she wanted, and she generally used to clean two and a half dozen every night, they said, to have ready for breakfast next mornin'. But when she come out to camp Paul always had to ship in a few hundred dozen to have for her entertainment while she was there.

One time, when she was out one Saturday, she was down by the river watchin' a boom of logs the men was workin' on, and she wanted to go out on one of the logs just to see if she could do it, just for fun, she says.

And while she was out there on the end of the log, she happened to sneeze, and ker-plunk! went both her jaws of false teeth in the water.

Well, there was considerable screamin' and yellin', I can tell you, and Mrs. Paul was cryin', for the first time in her life, they said, for she didn't never expect to see her teeth again, and they had been made special for her by Krupps' Iron Works, in Germany, and she didn't know how she'd ever get 'em replaced. Nobody couldn't go out and get them, because the men's boots, though they was high, wasn't high enough for anybody to wade out that far.

Well, about that time Paul come along, and Mrs. Paul was there, wailin' and screamin' of course: "Oh, my teeth! my teeth!"

And Paul stood there lookin' down at the teeth layin' down there at the bottom of the river with the water ripplin' over them, and he stood scratchin' his head for a while, and then finally he goes away without sayin' a word, and pretty soon we seen him comin' down the road with a piece of cable in one hand and somethin' else in the other, and when he come nearer, we seen it was a chicken drumstick.

Well, everybody was watchin', and wonderin' what he was goin' to do, naturally, and listenin' to Mrs. Paul wailin' around.

And what Paul done was, he just went ahead and fastened that drumstick he'd brought to the piece of cable and then went out on the log and lowered it in the water right in front of the teeth, and when them teeth sees that drumstick they

HE . . . LOWERED IT IN THE WATER RIGHT IN FRONT OF THE
TEETH

just naturally snaps right onto it. And Paul hauled 'em up, and so then Mrs. Paul was all fixed again.

Paul had a daughter, Teeny, that maybe I've mentioned before, and also a son. Mrs. Paul gave the boy an ax to play with one day and he cut his teeth on it. Paul told me himself that he didn't hardly dare to look at the boy when he was down at the ranch, because every time he looked at him he seemed to of growed a foot taller.

Teeny, the girl, used to be around the camp a good deal when she was little, they said, and I guess the men used to like her, for she was a mighty cute little thing. And one time she saved her father's life.

Paul was tryin' out a new circle saw in his shingle mill one forenoon and was so interested he forgot to come in when the dinnerhorn blowed, and they sent Teeny out to look for him.

Well, she found him, but the sawdust was up over his ears already, and it was pilin' up so fast he come pretty near bein' choked to death, and she dug him out all by herself, by tunnelin' under first and lettin' in some air, and then diggin' away the tunnel.

Paul was mighty proud of her for it. "Dug in and had her father out in just no time," he said.

Once he give her the job of bringin' home the eggs for the camp for a couple of seasons. She generally planted the egg-plant on a hill, and then she could roll home on the eggs and have 'em all beat up when she got there, ready to go in the cake, and then she'd always take the shells back and have 'em re-filled again for the next time.

And she had some hens too, to lay eggs for her. One time she got an egg so big they had to flatten it on both ends to get it through the cook-house door.

A tinware drummer that happened to be there wanted to know what kind of a hen it was that laid that size of egg, and Teeny told him that there wasn't no hen could lay an egg like that alone, it took a whole flock of 'em.

Teeny growed up mighty fast and got to be a big husky girl like her mother, with blue eyes and freckles, and mighty fond of coffee, like her dad. When she was just turned seventeen Ole the Blacksmith begun courtin' her and the cook used to invite him in sometimes to drink a little snack of coffee with Teeny in the afternoon. But I guess Ole thought she was pretty fine, though.

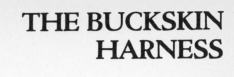

THE BUCKSKIN HARNESS

SUPPOSE everybody's seen pictures of the big log loads we used to haul in the woods in the old times. Loads piled up, ten or twelve rows of logs on top of each other, and the teamster standin' alongside the load, and the top log way up in the air there above his head, and I can tell you them pictures ain't no exaggeration nor nothin' out of the ordinary. Three or four times as high as a man's head I've seen them loads many times. Naturally you had to have a good top-loader to get 'em that high, but that was the top-loader's business to be a good top-loader, and if he knowed what he was about he knowed how to build 'em as high as you'd a mind to have 'em.

In Paul's camp, though, we had 'em higher'n any you could ever of seen in any of the pictures. They used to be so high we had to have a telephone to phone up to the loader, and

noon-time they always sent his dinner up to him in a balloon.
Generally he used to write a letter before he went up in the
mornin' to send to his mother in case he shouldn't never come
down again.

Course they couldn't of drawed them big loads if it hadn't
of been for the buckskin harness that was invented about that
time. That come in just before Paul went into Minnesota to
log in them big white pine woods there. He used to hitch up
Babe by Lake Vermilion and then the logs would be drawed
down to Duluth or Two Harbors in one pull.

Everybody knows how buckskin stretches when it gets wet,
and then shrinks all up to nothin' almost when it gets dry and
warm in the sun. Well, that's the principle the buckskin harness was invented on, and the same as with many inventions,
I guess, it was invented practically by pure accident. Look at
the way Watt invented the steam engine, just watchin' an old
teakettle boil.

But I was goin' to tell about the buckskin harness, and the
way that come to be invented was, one of the bull-cooks was
goin' to haul the wood in for the cook-house stove. They'd
used up all the wood that was near by already, and so he had
to go out a good ways out in the woods to get it. The cook was
a pretty cranky feller and he'd told him he'd better bring
home something dry that would burn if he knowed what was
good for him, and so the bull-cook took his ox and went away
over to the south of the camp where the burnt-over land was.
Figgured some of them burnt trunks would be dry on the
inside anyway. It was rainin' pitchforks that mornin' and
nothin' couldn't happen to be dry on the outside by any way
or chance.

The ox he had was a big one, though of course not big like Babe, and he had a bran new buckskin harness on him.

And so when he got there he cut down a couple of dozen burnt trees and put the logs on the sled and then he starts out for home with 'em, over the trail. First part of it was just kind of a narrow sled-track through the woods, but about half way that road turned out on one of the big main loggin' roads. He was glad he hit that part of the road and from there on he drove a little faster, walkin' along beside the ox and not botherin' to look back any. And course it was rainin' all the time hard as ever.

Well, when he got to camp it was about noon, and he drove his ox up right close to the door back of the cook-house, and then when he turned around he seen he didn't have no load at all, but the harness was stretched out all the way down the road to the big tree where the turn was, where the log trail went into the woods, and he knowed his load of stove wood must be somewheres down there behind the tree standin' there. He was just goin' to start back and get it when the dinnerhorn commenced to toot, and he calculated he might as well go in and eat his dinner and go and tend to his load afterwards.

"That'll be the best thing I can do," he says.

And then while he was eatin' his dinner and while all of the rest of us was eatin' dinner, the sun come out.

And so, in about fifteen minutes, when the bull-cook come back out again, there was his load of wood standin' there right in front of him, and pretty near climbin' up on the old ox's back, so he had to holler for help and hurry and cut him loose before it went right up on top of him.

You know, what happened was, when the sun come out, that buckskin harness had begun to shrink. And that's how it had pulled the load up by itself, without the ox doin' no pullin' at all on his part.

One of the cookees called Paul to see it, and Paul took out a patent on the harness, and the buckskin harness was used for all long hauls in Paul's camp ever since. A fine invention, you see, that come about that way, only the sun hadn't dried out the wood enough, and the cook swore at the bull-cook just the same, like as if he hadn't tried to do his best.

Paul did some great loggin' in Minnesota. Them forests up there was sure fine forests—stretches of pine and spruce and hemlock, with sometimes some white birches in between. Get up on a rise and you could see them all below you like a great

ocean, big dark waves where the spruce was, and light patches of jack pine climbin' up on the hills, and the red willows that used to grow along the cricks. Paul used to climb up on Jasper Point sometimes just to enjoy the sight of it, and at the same time to make sure that the three rivers that make their start there was doin' their job of keepin' his three loggin' operations apart—he'd put 'em in on purpose for that, so he wouldn't get 'em mixed up. They're the Nelson-Saskatchewan, you know, and the St. Lawrence and the Mississippi. Jasper Point is the height of land between 'em.

Paul always liked it in Minnesota, though. There was plenty of Swedes around all the time that he could get hold of to work for him whenever he wanted, and then the huntin' was good in them there woods too.

One time, I know, Paul went huntin' spruce patridges. And he hadn't got out in the woods very far yet and hadn't been lookin' around very long till all of a sudden he seen 540 of 'em sittin' in a row on a spruce bough, and he begun figgurin' how was the best way to get 'em.

Course he had his shotgun along and his rifle too, and with

his shotgun he could of got 'em all, because there was just enough shot in the load for one shot for each patridge, but he didn't like to get 'em that way if he could help, because he knowed they would be so much trouble to pick up afterwards each one by itself that way.

So what he done was, he took his rifle and went over to the end of the limb and fired and sent the bullet right through the length of the limb and split it open all the way to the tree, and then, just as he figgured, the patridges all got their toes caught in the rebound in the crack he'd made and stuck fast. And then he reloaded his rifle, leavin' the ramrod in, and shot that right through all the patridges. That way he got all but four that he didn't get quite big enough a hold on to make 'em stick on the rod.

He'd finished that shot, and had just turned round, when he seen a fine big buck standin' there not so very far away. He fired his shotgun at him quick and he seen the buck tumble over the ledge just as he fired.

It was such a fine carcass he couldn't hardly wait to get there to get hold of it, so he run as fast as he could to the place where the buck had been. Well, he run too fast. Result was, he run faster than the load, and got ahead of it, and got the whole charge of buckshot in his own back. For the buck'd got scared to death when he seen Paul, and hadn't waited for the shot to reach him.

Ole the Blacksmith come out and helped Paul back to camp and carried the patridges and the buck in for him. The buck when dressed weighed nine hundred seventy-five pounds.

There in Minnesota, the Minneapolis millmen used to want peeled logs, and Paul never liked that much. Oh, there was

HE RUN FASTER THAN THE LOAD

some sense to it, I spose—would keep the logs from rottin' if they had to lay in the water a long time—but not much—Paul always said it was nothin' but fol-de-rol, and I think he was about right. Anyway, it used to make him all-fired plaguy mad. The way he'd peel 'em when he got mad, he'd just hitch the Blue Ox to 'em and jerk 'em out whole. Even, he didn't bother to cut the trees down sometimes but just pulled 'em out from the top, so he got the heart out and left the limbs and bark standin'. That way a good deal was wasted, of course, and it was a lot of trouble, because he couldn't do but one at a time. I don't know how mad he would of got, but they quit askin' for 'em after a while—maybe the sawmill men heard how Paul felt about it, and thought they'd better not ask to get peeled logs no more.

What Paul liked best to do was a whole lot of trees at a time. There in Minnesota he got himself a long fallin' saw that would reach across half a mile or more. Of course if the country was a little hilly or there was a hollow or rise of ground, it didn't work so good, because they'd just get the tops of the trees that growed down in the hollows and up on the hills the saw would hit in the ground and get dulled on the rocks. Paul had to keep a gang of two hundred filers to keep that saw filed. And that was the saw that Paul always pulled one end of himself. He didn't care who pulled the other end, and he didn't care if they'd ride the saw, he said, if they felt like it, but what he didn't want was for 'em to drag their feet—he drawed the line on that.

Paul always liked to do things on a big scale. One of his ways was just to hitch Babe onto a whole section of timber at a time and haul it into camp and clear it off. If he got one in about sundown, after the day's work was over, he'd generally get it all cleared before supper.

That was efficient so far as the time it took was concerned anyway. But he couldn't of done it without Babe to haul it in for him.

Like one of these here efficiency experts would say, the overhead cost and maintenance for Babe was high, but on account of low operatin' expense and great efficiency, he was pretty economical camp equipment. And Paul couldn't of done much without him, I know that.

Like the time when they drove the wrong logs down the river and over the St. Anthony Falls; Babe just drank the river dry above the falls and sucked 'em all back again.

THE WINTER OF THE BLUE SNOW

NE of the worst winters I ever put in with Paul—or anywhere, for that matter—was the winter of the Blue Snow. It was so cold that winter that the loggers all swore blue streaks, and the snow all turned blue—came down blue in the first place, and then turned bluer after it touched the ground, too. The women down in the settlements used to use a little of it for blue in their blue-water, and whenever cows happened to get some of it along with the dry grass they was eatin', they gave blue milk.

It was sure a pretty sight too, though you couldn't hardly forget the cold long enough to stop and look at it. Blue, blue everywhere, as far as the eye could see, stretchin' along to the west in the open places, and in the woods around the trees, a little mound around each one with just a little hole in the middle around where the tree was.

The two Joe Murphys—brothers—one of 'em named Pete
—had the job of holdin' up the skylines in camp that winter,
and I used to help 'em sometimes—so I seen a good deal of
the snow—more'n my share, likely.

It was a hard job we had, for the snow was so nearly the
same color as the sky, that you couldn't hardly tell sometimes
where one left off and the other begun—like the time we was
layin' out the ice-road round a big hill in order to get away
from the grade. We'd been workin' for about a week or so,
and then all of a sudden one mornin' we come out and the hill
was all gone, and all it'd been was a big cloud we'd been
tryin' to work around. And that way it was hard all right, and
walkin' around in it up over our shoes and rubbers every day
wasn't what you might call comfortable neither.

And there was the snow-snakes—that was the worst of it
that winter. All over the ground, no matter where you went,
there was them snakes crawlin' around, and you couldn't
hardly get away from them, for they'd coil up and jump at
you if you wasn't careful—and a bite was almost always sure
death. Freeze to death, naturally—and then the only thing
that could save you was a good drink of whisky if that happened to be handy. Otherwise you was done for and you had
to learn to be more careful another time.

And the little pesky frost-biters up in the hills was pretty
bad, too, though not quite so bad as the snakes—but they'd
worry you a lot more.

It was sure cold that winter. It was so cold that the words
froze in our mouths when we tried to talk and Paul had to
send to England for a frozen word interpreter. Some of the
combinations that come out that spring when they begun to

thaw out—I tell you, you'd know then what somebody thought of you, all right.

One fellow that talked an awful lot the words froze so thick around him that Paul finally had to get the Blue Ox to haul him out at last. And the green bull-cooks froze in their tracks every time Paul spoke to 'em.

Yes, and it was cold inside, in the cook-shanty and the bunkhouse, too. If I had 'em here, I could get twenty men to swear if I could get one, that the coffee that was served in camp that winter used to be froze stone cold before the flunkies could get half way down the tables with it. Though, for that matter, that wasn't no uncommon thing other winters. And the icicles on the beards used to be pretty near as long some of the other winters, too—it wasn't so very different in that respect.

One mornin' Paul was goin' to town and he went to make him some hot coffee before he started out, and I'll be blamed if he didn't find the coffee-pot froze solid to the back of the stove, and even Paul couldn't budge it.

Ice froze so fast that winter, it froze warm and was too hot to handle. And Lake Superior froze solid to the bottom. In the spring Paul had to haul the ice all up on the shore to thaw it out, and then he had to re-stock the lake with new fish.

I know myself—just to show how cold it was—from actual experience; I was sittin' by the stove one evenin' takin' off my shoes. When I went to get up to hang up my socks, I wasn't able to make it without the bench I had been sittin' on follerin' me—stuck tight. And what'd happened was, somebody'd spilled water on it before I sat down, and it had froze solid to the seat of my pants, and stuck there till I could get some of the boys to pry it off of me. That's how cold it was in the bunkhouse actually that winter.

And all that time I'd been sittin' right up close to the stove as close as I could get, and pretty near roastin' on the front of me; for there was a big fire burnin' so the stove-pipe was red up to the roof pretty near.

We had to have a lot of whisky in camp that winter of the Blue Snow, naturally, for, like I said, that was the only remedy that would help in case of a bite from the snow-snakes. And you'd have to get it quick too—you couldn't stand to stand around and wait for it very long.

And so Paul—he was pretty nice about anythin' like that and tried to take good care of his men always—had a big trough put up, and that was kept full all the time, and a dipper hangin' by always handy, but even that wasn't enough. There used to be so many around all the time, and then besides it was hard to get the supply to fill the barrel, and Paul didn't hardly know what to do.

"I don't know where to get any more from," he says.

But then finally something happened one day that helped him out.

You see there was a fellow in camp that time called Sour-Face Murphy. And he was sour—sour enough to turn anythin'. And one day one of the cookees was peelin' a mess of spuds in the sink.

He was pretty near through and was just goin' to take 'em out, when he seen all of a sudden the whole mess of peelin's turnin' sour. And he looked up to see what had happened, and there was Sour-Face Murphy standin' in the door, and that's what'd done it.

Well, he fished the peelin's all out, and there in the bottom of the sink was twenty gallons of whisky as good as you'd ever want to get. And so Sam, the cook, went and told Paul about it, and Paul, who'd been wantin' to get some whisky from somewheres, and anyway was always lookin' for new and better improvements to use in camp, took Sour-Face off the load gang right away and turned him into camp distillery, and so we had all the whisky we ever wanted or had any kind of use for after that. And then the snow-snake trouble was better too, so there wasn't any more casualties that I know of, the last part of the winter.

One way that the men protected themselves from the cold was by raisin' long beards. Good growths of beard was pretty generally the style in the loggin' camps any time, but that winter of the Blue Snow they was extra long. They was so long that they covered the men pretty near all the way from the chin to the toes. The ends the men tucked in their boots, one half in each felt boot, sittin' generally on the edge of their bunks to do it. Some of 'em got 'em in too tight and then there was danger of makin' themselves humpbacked, but that wasn't dangerous to most, because they was too long, the beards, I mean. Out in the woods the wind used to whistle through 'em, so you couldn't hardly tell whether it was the beards or the tops of the pine trees that made that singin' that you heard.

In the spring when the weather got warm and they didn't need their beards for protection no more, and they was gettin' in the way anyway, the men had 'em all cut off. We used our axes for the first few cuts—course they had to be sharpened up good—and that way they could do it for each other—and then to finish up the job we went at it the reggelar way with razors. Of course that don't mean Paul. He couldn't never use a common size razor, naturally—a good sharp scythe is what he always used.

The whiskers that was cut off was all stacked up in haystacks, and Paul sent down for somebody to come up and make him a price, and one of the McAdam Mattress Company's men come up and dickered for and bought the whole lot.

I don't know why the whiskers growed so good that winter unless it was the cold. Fur animals always has thicker fur in cold winters than in mild ones. And then the whisky the men drunk might of done somethin' to it—they naturally always spilled a good deal.

Well, that was the Winter of the Blue Snow, but I mustn't forget the Spring of the Deep Mud that come after it, for where the snow'd been six foot deep that winter, the mud, that spring, was sixty times six foot, like the Good Book says. And the ice-roads stood up twenty foot out of a lake of mud on each side.

That's the way them ice-roads was, though, generally. Built of solid ice that way and packed down good, they wouldn't melt down near so fast as the snow on the sides, and in the spring pretty near always they'd be standin' up high that way, long after most of the other snow and sleddin' was all gone.

A warm day come about the middle of April that year and the soft snow melted away in just about a single day.

There'd been a crust up on top of it—a January thaw we'd had, and then a stiff freeze right after it so the crust'd formed, and most of the skiddin' that winter had been done up on that crust. And so when it melted away quick like that in the

WE USED OUR AXES FOR THE FIRST FEW CUTS

spring, in the places where the snow'd been deepest, the skid sleds was standin' right up in the treetops the next mornin'.

And then it kept right on thawin' the next few days and I tell you the mud there got to be along that loggin' road was somethin' awful. By one of the crossin's, especially.

One of the teamsters was comin' by there with a load just about dark one evenin' and he slipped in right by the crossin', and it wasn't but a minute or two till he was all covered over way up to the cattle's noses.

Another teamster, about two miles further back on the road, heard their last bellow that they made, and so hurried up to help 'em.

This teamster pried the cattle's head out of the mud and got a chain around one of 'em's horns and hitched onto that and started to haul.

"Hold on there, Ed," he hollered, "I can get you out all right."

But of course you might know what happened was, when he was tryin' to haul crosswise that way, and the road slippery like it was, he slid off into the mud hole on the other side. But that automatically helped the first one out, of course, and he started to haul the other fellow out, but then he slipped in again a second time, naturally, and I don't know how long that would of kept up and they might be goin' yet, see-sawin' back and forth that way, but Brimstone Bill happened to come along just then leadin' the Blue Ox, and he hitched onto the chain halfway between the two other yokes of cattle, and so hauled 'em both down the loggin' road and into camp.

N THE winters Paul used to do some great huntin' alongside of his lumberjackin' —just kind of as a side line—I think I mentioned once before the big gun he had, and huntin' patridges that day. It wasn't no trouble to him ever. When he went out cruisin' of a Sunday he might as well take a gun along and see what he could get. Sort of kill two birds with one stone. He didn't let it interfere with his loggin' none. And comin' home along the loggin' road of an evenin' if he met a pack of wolves he might as well get a few of 'em and get the bounty, him as well as anybody else. He had the Wisconsin state treasury pretty near broke one winter payin' him bounties.

The way he got the wolves was, he just scared 'em to death hollerin' at 'em. He used to holler so loud when he was a kid, he could kill a whole pondful of bullfrogs with one holler. So now when he met them timber wolves on the road he'd just catch 'em by the ears and holler down their throats till they died of fright, and then he'd tie their ears in a bow knot and string the carcasses over his fingers and carry 'em home to camp that way for the bounty.

For real huntin' Paul used to load his gun with railroad spikes—till Jim Hill got so prosperous he bought 'em all up so Paul couldn't get no more—and for small game like squirrels and rabbits he generally used bits of haywire cut up in about inch pieces. The spikes was good because if he shot 'em lengthwise like he generally did they made a deep clean hole and didn't cut the meat up none.

Paul had a big huntin' dog called Elmer that he took along for big game. Elmer had an extra long nose so he could get the scent of most anythin', and short ears that stood straight out away from his head so he always could hear good.

One winter—it was about the third or fourth winter I was with Paul and we was loggin' on the south shore of Lake Superior, I remember—some big stories come in to camp about a buck that was frequentin' the woods around there in upper Wisconsin and Michigan. Two of the teamsters said they saw him one day along the loggin' road and if what they said was true, the stories we was hearin' about him wasn't exaggerated none.

Well, Paul didn't wait to hear the story the teamsters told but onct till he made up his mind he'd go out and get that buck. And so he loads his gun with a couple of kags of spikes and a barrel or so of powder and calls Elmer to follow him and away he goes.

They hunted all the way down to Detroit that mornin' and

around by Flint and up north again, and Paul could see by the tracks that it was a big buck.

About the middle of the afternoon they got hot on the buck's trail and Elmer was already beginnin' to sniff more interested-like and let out a bark or two, and they would of had the buck in no time, they was so close to him, only just then an occurrence happened that delayed Paul and give the buck a chance to get away, for the time bein' anyway.

You see, one of the farmer boys that lived on one of them stump ranches in the neighborhood of the camps had been roamin' around in the woods lookin' for squirrels and he'd fell into one of that there buck's tracks. Paul always had a good heart in him and naturally couldn't leave the boy to drown very well there in that hole; so he stopped and fished him out.

"I was just tryin' to get on the same side of the tree as the squirrel," the kid says.

And Paul had to stop for a few minutes extra to show the
kid the proper way to hunt squirrels, and that's how he used
up some more time and lost the trail of the buck again for a
while.

Toward evenin' though they succeeded in catchin' up with
him again and Paul brought him down with his gun with
one shot. He was mighty proud, for it was the biggest animal
he'd ever killed yet. About twice as big as the one he'd killed
down on Maple River that time.

He was standin' there lookin' down at the buck and thinkin'
what a fine shot he'd made when all at once he heard Elmer
makin' a queer noise, and he turned round and there was his
faithful hound takin' his last gasps. Paul noticed that his
tongue was stickin' two feet out of his mouth and his sides
was goin' up and down like a pair of bellows or like waves
on the ocean.

"Poor old dog," says Paul.

And he tried to help him up, but it was too late. Elmer had
been tuckered out by the chase of that day and died of heart
failure from overexertion.

So Paul sat down there by Elmer for a spell feelin' pretty
bad, when all at once he happened to remember that now he
was worse off than he'd thought he was before, for he
wouldn't know what in the world to do with all that meat,
and now he had two carcasses on his hands instead of one.

Just about that time, though, Mr. Armour happened to
come along from Chicago, and Paul sold the meat to him.
Armour give a million dollars for the buck carcass and a
thousand dollars for the dog carcass. That was the beginnin'

HE WAS ALWAYS RUNNIN' DOWNHILL

of the Armour meat packin' business.

Paul hadn't never knowed that Elmer was troubled with heart failure—he'd always seemed alright enough—and he was surprised and kind of didn't know what to think, when the meat had been taken away and there wasn't nothin' left and he knowed he'd lost his huntin' dog for good. But it had been a pretty fast hunt that day—all over Michigan and Wisconsin—and even Paul himself was still puffin' some when he come into camp that night.

Well, a few weeks after that when he'd kind of got over Elmer's loss a little, he started figgurin' on how he could get another dog, one that would be able to stand the pace, for he couldn't afford to slow up his huntin' none for the sake of a dog. Well, he got it figgured out finally.

What he done was, he made a cross between an extra short-legged Dachshund and one of these here Russian wolfhounds, that's got such awful long legs, you know. The pup, when he grew up, stood a little over seven axhandles behind and only two feet in front. That way, you see, like the way Paul had it figgured beforehand, he was always runnin' downhill and didn't have to get tired, and so it wasn't hard on his heart. It's a fact, that huntin' dog of Paul's could run for a week straight and never seem to feel it at all, but turn up fresh and smilin' for his supper at the cook-shanty after the hunt was over, waggin' his tail at the cook.

Paul accidentally tried another experiment on a dog that come pretty near turnin' out successful, but didn't quite.

He had a little terrier, Zip, that he used to take with him sometimes when he went out for fun of an afternoon. One day he and Zip was followin' a big he-bear. The bear was

amblin' along pretty fast and Zip was goin' lickety split after
him. All of a sudden the bear turned behind a tree, and Zip,
who was goin' so fast he couldn't stop, went slam into an ax
that Paul had left there standin' against the tree, and just
naturally split himself in two down the middle from end to
end.

Paul didn't waste no time, but hurried up and picked up
the pieces quick and slapped 'em together again before they
had a chance to get cold or bleed to death, and set the dog
back on the ground. But it was then he seen that while tryin'
to hurry he'd put 'em together wrong, and two of Zip's legs
was stickin' up and two down. Zip started off on his two
right legs and could run most as fast as he could on four, and
when those two got tired he turned himself over and run on
the other two. That way half of him could be restin' all the
time, naturally.

It might of been a very good invention, only Zip's brains
and legs didn't work together as well as they should of, and
so sometimes his two left legs would get started runnin' backwards and would run back as far as the right legs had run
forward and the poor dog'd be back in the same place from
where he had started from.

For to have a big dog to run along beside the Blue Ox when
he was draggin' a load down the road and kind of look nice
and be of a size to match the Ox, Paul figgured to cross a
Saint Bernard with a Canada moose. The pup was a big one—
about the size of a good-sized steer when he was born—and
Paul had him nursed on bear's milk so he'd grow fast.

He was a pretty dog, with a broad forehead like a moose,
and gentle eyes and a blackish-blue nose and long brown hair

and quite a nice round back with a good layer of fat under it. He would certainly of looked nice when he'd got a little bigger, trottin' down the ice-roads between the trees behind the Blue Ox, or a little in front of him maybe, if he felt like it, but Paul had bad luck with that dog. It was too bad. You could hardly think it would of happened that way. After an extra big dinner of bear's milk one day that pup was drowned fallin' through six foot of ice on Lake Superior. And Paul never felt like tryin' to get a road dog again after that.

But the dog of Paul's that everybody knowed best was Nero, the one he kept in camp always, and he was sure a fierce brute. Paul had that dog, I know, as long as I knowed him, and I don't know but what he took him to Alaska with him when he went up there.

The oldtimers used to scare the young farmer boys and student bull-cooks that come to camp by tellin' them that Paul kept that dog to sic on the swampers in the spring when they had a winter's pay comin', so they wouldn't dare ask for their money, but would be glad enough just to get out of the way with their lives. But of course that wasn't so, anyone might know that.

Paul was a kind-hearted man, and a fair and square boss if he was anythin', and he wouldn't of held a man's wages back on him, nor he wouldn't sic a dog onto him neither. What Paul kept Nero for was to feed the watch peddlers, and the coffee and hardware drummers, and the camp inspectors to when they come to camp. Paul kept Nero fierce on purpose so he'd have a good appetite for them pests, and he growed fiercer because he ate 'em—it worked both ways naturally.

That other dog, Skookum, that could run downhill, Paul took West with him when he come out. I don't know what ever become of him, but you'll find the loggers all know about him. Ask any of 'em if they knowed Paul's dog Skookum and they'll tell you. He was a great dog all right.

LOGGING
NORTH DAKOTA

PAUL had just finished loggin' Minnesota when the letter from the king come.

The king of Sweden had heard of Paul from some of the Swedes that had come back after havin' been loggin' with him over here, I spose, and that's how he happened to write to Paul, or maybe he had just naturally heard about him anyway—I don't know, but anyway he wrote to him and asked him to help him out.

He'd had a lot of onruly socialists in his country, it seems, and about that time they was gettin' too many for him— more'n he could handle. Always wantin' to improve things, he says, and never willin' to let good enough alone. And now it'd got so bad it'd just about got to the point of "Ship or Shoot" with him—he just naturally couldn't do nothin' with 'em no more.

He didn't like to shoot, because that always looks bad in the papers, and so he figgured he'd better ship, and that's the way it come he wrote to Paul. He'd heard what kind of a logger Paul was, of course, and his idea was to try to get him to clear a piece of land for him where he could send his people and where they could settle and be prosperous and never have to come back.

Well, Paul got the letter one afternoon when the tote-teamster brought the mail, and I guess he could tell by the size and by the gold trimmin' all around it that it was somethin' important. And so he got the timekeeper to read it to him like usual and then when they'd read it they read it through again, and then Paul says, "Sure, I guess I can do that all right."

And then he went over to Charley Dobey and he says to Charley: "What do you think of that country we seen when we was out cruisin' last Sunday? That ought to suit 'em, don't you think? Here's the letter," he says. "That's what I'm talkin' about."

And when Charley'd got through readin' it, Paul says to him, "I'm goin' to have you write the answer for me. I ain't goin' to have Johnny Inkslinger write it. He goes too fast."

That chief clerk of Paul's sure was a fiend for speed and economy. One winter he left off dottin' his i's and crossin' his t's and saved nine barrels of ink that way. He wrote with a fountain pen that he had connected up with a barrel of ink, so he could go right on and never stop till the barrel was empty, and then only for a minute or two while he changed the hose. And every time he charged the men for tobacco or socks from the commissary he used a split pencil to double charge their accounts, and so made money for the boss. And Johnny was sure the speediest at mixin' up a walk for a feller of anybody I ever saw, and you know, I guess, most of 'em was pretty swift at that.

But Paul didn't want Johnny to write this letter for him, because he was afraid he would go too fast and make a mistake, and so he got Charley to write it for him. Charley could write and cipher about the best of anybody in camp, and he was always the one that the men used to get to write their letters for 'em, when they was sick or in trouble or had to write to their girls or somethin'. Sometimes he'd be busy all Sunday afternoon that way. They could always trust Charley because he never had anything to do with the girls and they knowed he wouldn't try to take 'em away from 'em, like some of them that wrote letters for the others always used to try to do. Charley was a partikkelar friend of mine and he showed me the letter he wrote to the king that time for Paul, and it went somethin' like this if I remember right:

DEAR KING:

Answerin' to your letter about a place for them subjects of yours. Everybody knows the proper place for Swedes is North Dakota. I can use 'em in my loggin'.

If I put Babe on the job it won't take long. I want 400,000 more please. Course the logs won't do you no good so I'll keep 'em. Begin next week.

Yours truly,
PAUL BUNYAN.
his (X) mark

Charley had to write the name in for him, and drawed a picture of the Blue Ox for a kind of trade-mark, and Paul made just an X under his name, for Paul couldn't read nor write. He hadn't never learned, for I guess he hadn't never went to school more than that one half day that time. But most times it didn't make no difference anyway—a man can be a pretty good lumberjack even if he don't know how to write. For keepin' his accounts Paul generally made notches in a tree outside the cook-shanty door, and when he wanted anything he most generally made a picture of it and got it that way.

But one time he made a pretty bad mistake, though—that was the time when the double-jawed feller had chawed up the camp grindstone. Paul was goin' to send for one and he made a picture of it and gave it to the tote-teamster to bring out for him.

Well, when the tote-teamster come back and we went through all the things he'd bought there wasn't no grindstone there, but down on the bottom there was a great big cheese, that nobody didn't seem to've ordered. And so we knowed something was wrong.

What'd happened was, when Paul made the picture of the grindstone he forgot to put in the square hole in the middle of it, and so that's how they'd come to make a mistake and thought it was a cheese instead.

Well, that was one time. But generally it was all right, and Paul got what he wanted without no trouble. He wasn't mad, neither, that time. Just laughed, and thought it was a pretty good joke on himself. Paul was a pretty good-natured man, most times, unless somebody made him mad by not knowin' nothin', like Pete Legoux.

Well, Paul didn't have but the one winter to clear North
Dakota in, and the loggin' he did there was as great loggin'
as I ever seen him do. Course he used more new-fangled
methods afterwards and bigger maybe, but never no better; for
that was a fine camp we had, and some fine loggin' that was
done there in North Dakota.

"I'm goin' to do a good job," he says. "Seein' as how the
king's heard I can log, we're goin' to do some real loggin'
this time, and we're goin' to have a camp, too."

And we did, all right. The Pyramid Forty'd been great, and
loggin' in Minnesota hadn't been no slouch neither, but it
wasn't nothin' compared to this camp in North Dakota. That
was ten times bigger'n anything he'd ever done before, and a
good number of times better.

The plan for the camp was pretty much the same as he'd
always used. Nothing much new, or new-fangled, but only
a good deal bigger.

The hotcake griddle, f'rinstance, was just like the hotcake
griddle we'd had in Michigan, and he got it from Moline
again, but he drove Babe on the run comin' to camp and so
got much more speed in it this time, so when it come to spin-
the-plate it made a much bigger furnace for under itself than
it had done before, and set itself down in the ground quite a
good ways too—and that made it better, naturally.

Paul had six concrete-mixers put up around it and a sixty-
foot tank for each mixer for a reservoir, and traveling cranes
to put the batter in with, and he had an engine and a steam
whistle to give the signal when the flunkies was to get out of
the way.

Instead of twenty men with slabs of bacon on their feet skatin' around greasin' the griddle, Paul had eighty now.

After a while, a little ways along in the winter, they didn't make them big hotcakes no more, but made a whole lot of little fellows instead, and that was better. They was handier in a good many ways, too. The cook would string 'em up on haywire, f'rinstance, and make 'em up in rings, and then the waiters could ride along on horseback and sling a bunch to each man as they galloped along.

That way we could make much better time at breakfast and always be out in the woods long before daylight. Some of the men used to say Paul thought so much of them, that that's why he had to get 'em up in the middle of the night to feed 'em.

Many's the time, let me tell you, I've seen the stars go down and the sun come up out in the woods. That was the regular thing in the old camps always. Some of the men tried to get Paul to put up another moon so's they could see to chop on both sides of the tree, but they couldn't never get him to do that, though.

Yes, and then about the hotcakes. Babe used to be fond of them little fellers too. Seems like he could get his tongue round 'em better and he was gettin' crazier and crazier for hotcakes all the time. We might of knowed how it would end up, but naturally we didn't, then.

The stove in the cook-house in the camp in North Dakota was so big it took three acres of timber every day to keep the fire goin' in it. One day one of the cooks put some bread in the oven and went round to the other side to look at it, but it was so far around it'd baked and burned to a crisp before he

could get there. And another time another one of Sam's helpers got lost between the flour bin and the root cellar and would
like to of starved to death if somebody hadn't found him.

The tables in the dinin' room was covered with brown oil-
cloth, and was so long that Paul had to have waiters on roller-
skates to get the food down to the lower end before it would
be all eaten up by them that was lucky enough to be at the
upper end of the table. They had fish-nets to put the knives
and spoons in to swab 'em round and wash 'em, and Sam

always used a pitchfork to feel and see if the spuds was done.

There was one feller whose job it was to drive the salt and pepper wagons around the tables. He'd generally start out in the mornin' and get to the lower end at night, and he'd be ready to start back next mornin' again. That way he could make three trips a week. And a brother of his used to drive the saleratus wagons—that is one of 'em that did—there was four in all drivin' for Sam—and another brother from the same family had the job of pointin' the toothpicks.

Paul didn't find no hot spring handy in Dakota to cook the pea-soup in, the way he'd done back in Wisconsin, but there was a lake there not so far from the camp and he fired the slashin's around it, after he'd dumped the oxen and peas in, and it cooked just about as good—and of course, then there was more of it. The cookees sailed Mississippi stern-wheelers around in the lake to keep the soup stirred, and Paul had pipes put in and piped to different parts of the woods under ground so they could have artesian wells almost anywheres in the state and get the soup when they wanted it. The Standard Oil's got some of them pipes now.

So you can see then how everything was bigger in this camp than Paul had ever had before. But there was one thing Paul tried to have bigger that he got too big, though, so he couldn't use it on account of that—or only once anyway. And that was the dinnerhorn. It was so big that the first time Paul blowed on it he felled four acres of timber, and afterwards when he blowed straight up in the air he filled pretty near the whole Mississippi valley with wind and he didn't dare blow no more. It was an entire total loss—and all the tin and all the labor

Ole had put on it. Paul sent it East, where they used it for a tin roof on the railroad depot in Washington.

Like he had before, Paul had all the flour and beans and peas and prunes shipped in to camp by the trainload, but he had a cattle ranch up in Alberta himself from where he got the steers for the meat. They used to get in about two thousand steers at a shipment. That would last the camp a day or two.

Paul got the water for his ice-roads in North Dakota from Lake Superior. Used the Blue Ox always, and a tank. All them thousand lakes up in Minnesota is nothin' but Babe's footprints where he used to travel with the tank. One day Babe slipped and the tank tipped over and sprung a leak, and that's what started the Mississippi River. Paul dug it out with a shovel so he'd have a good route for his log drive. Just went down the valley towards the Gulf of Mexico, throwing a shovelful of dirt on each side as he went along, and so that way he made the Rocky Mountains and the Alleghanies at the same time, just incidentally, as you might say.

They said it was the shovel he used on that Mississippi job that he wore afterwards for a watch charm, but I never believed that myself. What I think is that it was the one he used for diggin' the Little Big Horn, that he wore. Stands to reason, seems to me, it couldn't of been the one he dug the Mississippi with. I spose I could just as well of asked him about that watch charm some time—I seen him wearin' it often enough—but I never did.

That was great loggin' we done in North Dakota, though, like I said.

Out in the woods before daylight—out among the pines. There was skidways all over between the trees and Paul's loggin' roads cuttin' up the whole state nearly. And the sound of timber fallin', and the call of the loggers when they'd fall a tree: "Tim-m-mber-er! Down the line. Watch out!" I can't help it, but I always thought that a mighty pretty sound, and I do yet. "Tim-mm-ber! Dow-n the line!" Yes, and then of course, there was other sounds too—the teamsters swearin' and cussin' at their cattle, for instance—or horses—Paul used some horses in loggin' off North Dakota too. And we used to work so fast that often we'd be skiddin' right in front of the buckers, and so the buckers would have to be runnin' alongside the log and it would almost be down to the landin' before they'd get the last cut made. By spring North Dakota was a very different-lookin' country, let me tell you.

But of course gettin' the timber off was easy for Paul. It was when he got to thinkin' about them millions of stumps that he begun to worry a little bit. Most generally he'd just moved on and left the stumps and manure piles and old camp buildin's standin' there.

Course he could of hitched Babe onto 'em and yanked 'em out, but that would be slow work and kind of tedious for the

ONE BLOW WAS GENERALLY ENOUGH

Ox. So he'd been figgurin' on it for a long time, how he could do it. And then one day somethin' happened which give him an idea.

The way that was: Paul had four fellers oilin' on his watch, two hard-grease men and two soft-grease men, and they was generally onto their job—I knowed 'em, all four of 'em, well, and they was pretty good men too—and was generally punctual about havin' it wound every Christmas and the Fourth of July and keepin' it oiled up good. But that year they got the spring-fever or the cabin-fever or somethin', and got lazy and laid down on their jobs. And the result, you might know, was, the watch ran a hot-box on the main bearin' and the babbit melted and run down Paul's pants leg one day, and it made him all-fired plaguy mad. He was standin' near a big stump at the time and he hit the stump an awful blow with his fist while he called for them oiler fellers to come up and get their time, and afterwards when he'd got over bein' so mad he looked down and he seen he'd knocked the stump six foot below the ground; and then that was what give him the idea.

The next day he had one of the biggest trees we'd cut down in North Dakota hauled into camp with the Blue Ox and had Ole make him a mall, and then after that Paul'd go out for a couple of hours every mornin' and knock down stumps. One blow was generally enough to send 'em six or eight feet below the surface and then the holes could be filled in afterwards with the scrapers, and that way in a couple of weeks he had the whole state cleared and smooth and that's why you don't find no stumps in North Dakota today anywheres.

Anywhere you look it's just as level and fine as a table top.

Only they say in Devil's Lake there's queer things come bob-
bin' up sometimes, and some say it's them old stumps of Paul's
that come out there. Naturally, I don't know. For one thing,
I ain't never been back to North Dakota since the winter I
logged with Paul there, though I always intended to, and I
may yet some day if things happen to turn out that way.

PAUL BUNYAN'S CORN-STALK

ELL, then when Paul had logged all the trees off North Dakota and pounded all the stumps down and got the land all cleared and smooth, he thought he was done and finished with the job. But then this other letter from the king come. The king wrote over and wanted to know if the soil was fertile, and he said he wouldn't let the contract be called finished till Paul had proved that to his satisfaction. It wouldn't be no use to send his people over, he said, unless the soil was good, so's they could raise enough to eat and not have to starve to death or come back, which, like he'd said the other time, of course, he didn't want 'em to do.

And so Paul didn't hardly know what to do.

Course he himself knowed the soil was fertile—couldn't hardly help but be with a stand of timber on it like that—but how to prove that to the king, that was another kind of a job, and he was pretty considerably worried—for Paul, that is. And what the king asked was reasonable enough too, Paul thought, even though it wasn't really in the contract, and he wanted to do it up right, a little more if anything rather than a little less, that was the way with Paul always. And so he had to figgur up something else to do about it.

Course he might of sent Ole over with a sample—he carried enough around on his shoes generally—and let the king try it, but then Ole was needed right where he was. Babe might need shoein' for one thing, and Ole was the only man in camp that could shoe him, and then besides there was Teeny—Paul didn't want him to get away from Teeny just then. Paul was tryin' to get Ole for a son-in-law, because Ole was about the best man he had, and he figgured if he could get him in the family that way he could always be sure of him and wouldn't have to raise his wages none to keep him. And so he didn't care to send him to a foreign country just then, where there might be pretty Swede girls around; but he had to think up some other way, if he could.

Well, what he finally figgured out was, he'd get some people to swear to affidavits for him. He'd plant something and then they'd watch it grow and swear to how far it growed the first day, and how far the second day, and how far the third day, and so on, all legal, and then they'd send the papers and the measurements to the king, and that ought to satisfy him.

So then when he'd got this all planned out and ready, Paul took a kernel of corn and went out and planted it.

Well, Paul, like I said, knowed that the soil there was

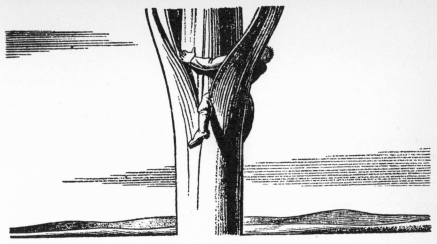

fertile, but not even he had any good idea of how fertile it was. And he hadn't no more'n turned around to go back to the camp to get Ole and the other men that was goin' to watch it, till that corn was up out of the ground and higher'n his knee already—and Paul'd planted it a good four foot deep in the hole he'd made with his little finger. And when him and Ole and Charley Nordstrom come runnin' out there it'd grew clean out of sight so you couldn't see the top at all no more.

Paul sent Ole up right away to cut the top off so it wouldn't grow no higher but it wasn't but a minute till Ole was pretty near clean out of sight too.

"Cut the top off so it'll branch out!" Paul yells up to where he thought Ole ought to be by that time. "Hurry up. Be quick."

"Can't do it, Paul!" Ole yells back. "Top no bin har. He grows so fast I cannint see him."

And Paul knowed it wasn't no use, for pretty soon they couldn't hardly see Ole no more, and Paul yells:

"Come on down then, Ole. Come on down!"

But Ole couldn't do that neither, because every foot he'd try to slide down, the cornstalk would carry him up three, it was growin' so fast, and so he kept goin' up and up all the time—good-by, Ole—and he would of starved to death if Paul hadn't of got his gun and shot him up some doughnuts and biscuits after a while.

And then Paul got his ax and tried to chop it down but he couldn't do that neither, because he couldn't never chop twice in the same place, the cornstalk was growin' so fast, and so he seen that wouldn't do.

Charley skooted back to camp and got two of the sawyers to come out and bring a saw and a couple of springboards— that was the first time springboards was used in the woods— but they couldn't do it with that neither. They got the spring-boards in all right, but by the time they got ready to get up on 'em they was too high, and they'd forgot to bring the top air extensions to their ladders, so that was no good.

And Paul was sure what you'd call up a tree, only it wasn't him that was up the tree but Ole, and that's what made Paul feel the worst. Teeny would take on pretty hard if she heard how Ole was goin' out of sight. Course he could comfort her with that he was goin' in the right direction anyway, but that wouldn't do her much good, for she'd rather have him on earth. And then besides there was his future loggin' opera-tions to take into consideration, for Ole he pretty near had to have for his loggin'. I think Paul dropped a tear out of the corner of one eye just about then, but it fell near the foot of the cornstalk and only made it grow faster.

So then Paul thought he maybe might get the Blue Ox and

"COME ON DOWN THEN, OLE. COME ON DOWN!"

try to pull the corn out by the roots, but he remembered he'd have to put the chain around the stem and it might grow tight to the stem, and then when Babe'd begin to pull it might carry him up with it, and he'd lose his Ox too, besides his blacksmith and maybe son-in-law. And so then he didn't hardly know what to do.

And just about that time one of them goverment inspectors

happened to come along.

"This your cornstalk?" he says to Paul.

"Well, I planted it," Paul says.

"You planted it. Well, then."

"I planted it," says Paul, "but I didn't make it grow."

"No matter," says the inspector. "It's your cornstalk. You will have to remove it."

"Uh, huh," grunted Paul.

"Law of Public Nuisances," explains the inspector. "This cornstalk of yourn is found to be a Public Nuisance. Agricultural farmers in lower Illinois and Iowa complains of shortage of water for their crops. Something, they say, is sucking away the water from under the soil and leaving their wheat crops high and dry. Not only that, but steamboat men on the Mississippi reports that the river has lowered six foot in the last six hours—"

"Well, I'll be darned," says Paul.

"Furthermore," says the inspector, puttin' on a legal way, like they do, "it is my duty to inform you that your cornstalk has to be cut down. For investigation has proved that it is that same cornstalk that is causing the disturbance complained of."

"Yah!" Kind of snappily from Paul.

"And the said owner of the said cornstalk is therefore directed to chop it down."

But at that Paul gets mad.

"That's what I been tryin' to do for the last six hours, you fool," he says. "Can't you see nothin'?"

"Law of Public Nuisances," keeps on the inspector. "I being the lawfully constituted—"

But he didn't get no further, for by the time he got that

big mouthful out of his mouth he was flyin' out over the edge of the field at the end of Paul's shoe. And Paul turns back to the cornstalk again.

"I got an idea," he says after a minute, after he'd been lookin' around for a little while.

What he done was, the Great Northern had been layin' a railroad through there not so very far away, and Paul got some of them railroad rails Jim Hill had left, and that's what he done it with. There was a big pile of them steel rails layin' there alongside the right-of-way and Paul just picks up a handful of 'em and brings 'em over to the cornstalk. He ties 'em all together in a long string and then with the help of the Blue Ox, that Charley had fetched, he swings 'em round the trunk of the corn and ties 'em in a knot.

With that, naturally, the corn begins to cut into itself, and it wasn't long before, growin' so fast, it'd cut itself clean through. With that steel rope around its neck, that cornstalk just naturally committed suicide, that's what it done.

And when it finally fell it took three days fallin', and made such a wind that the Mississippi valley's been full of wind storms and cyclones ever since.

Paul grubbed out the main part of the stump and you can see the hole standin' up three thousand feet in the air to this day. One of the ears of corn that was pretty near ripe struck into the ground when it fell down and they burnt out the cob afterwards and had a well two hundred foot down lined on all sides with roasted corn, just like they got a corn beef mine somewheres over in Montana too, that maybe you've heard of.

Well, Ole, when he seen the cornstalk was beginnin' to fall, climbed out on one of the blades and when he was pretty near the ground he just swung himself down like little boys swing down on saplings and naturally he wasn't hurt at all. He told Teeny afterwards she needn't to of worried none about his goin' clean through the sky and not bein' able to get back, because he had good suspenders on and they would of kept him from goin' clean through to the other side.

And the affidavits, and the king of Sweden. Well, Paul didn't get no affidavits, because nobody'd had time to take down any measurements, and there wasn't none that could be took down anyway, but a reporter on a Kansas paper wrote up the story, and Paul sent the clipping from the paper to the king. The Swede king believed the newspaper story all right because it was in print, you know, and so he sent all the money that was comin' to Paul, and then he sent his Swedes to North Dakota and there's where they are yet, a lot of 'em.

OFF FOR THE WEST

AUL BUNYAN was mighty proud of the job he'd done loggin' off North Dakota, and he used to like to stand out in front of the camp of a mornin' and admire the work he'd done, and keep jinglin' the money the Swede king had sent him in his pocket.

And so one Sunday mornin' he was standin' like that, lookin' around, and wonderin' where he'd be loggin' next, and thinkin' what a fine country it was stretching away out there to the west.

It was still early in the spring and there was a few patches of snow left in the low places and under the willows along the cricks; and other places the grass was sproutin' already, and the fields just laid there, ready for the plow to come in and turn it over and you could plant wheat or spuds or corn or anythin' else under the shinin' sun you'd a mind to.

"There," he says, "I guess that country is good enough for anybody, Swedes or Germans or Dutch or English—I don't care who—even Irish—and I reckon I earned my million dollars all right."

And he was leavin' the country, sure, as good, or a good deal better than he found it, and that's more than can be said for a good deal of loggin' that's done. It's a rotten shame the way they leave some of it, as if a cyclone had struck it, and never a stick would grow there no more. Just rocks and stumps and splinters, and young trees all tore up. Especially this high-lead loggin' that they do out here now.

Well, before him, like I said, was this fine green country he'd cleared, and behind him was the Red River of the North and the great broad valley both sides of it.

The way that river happened to be red, of course, you know, was the ketchup Al Peterson spilt in it. Al was one of the ketchup-drivers for the camp that winter and he drove his wagon over Paul's pipe one day that he'd laid down by the river bank, and so dumped his whole load. And that's what made the river red.

Brimstone Bill used to have Babe's barn right on the bank of the river too. Moved it every two or three days or so. That is, after Paul had put him wise to the trick of doin' it that way.

Bill was havin' the usual trouble, like always, keepin' the old Ox clean, and so Paul says to him one day:

"Why don't you move the barn, Bill? It would be cheaper and easier than tryin' to clean it, I'd think."

And so Bill did, and by the time we'd finished loggin' in the spring, the Red River valley was covered plum over and manured six foot deep, and there ain't no more fertile land nowhere than the Red River valley of the North.

Well, the way I was sayin', Paul had been figgurin' on where he was goin' to go next, and so then that mornin' he made up his mind.

"I'll go West," he says. "Reckon there'll be loggin' enough for me to do out there for a year or two anyway."

He'd heard about the Big Trees they had out there, and he'd seen the tops of some of 'em when he'd been out cruisin' one Sunday, and then Ole had told him about 'em too—he'd seen some of 'em from the top of the cornstalk the time he was up. And some fellows that had come into camp from the West told him about some outfit that was loggin' out there on the Coast on a big scale, and Paul, naturally, wanted to come out and show that fellow how to log.

And so he made up his mind to go right away.

Well, Paul happened to have his snowshoes on that mornin'. That may strike some folks as kind of funny, I spose, but Paul was always slow in layin' 'em off in the spring. Just the same as he was slow givin' up all the other things he'd used in the winter, too—like the loggin' road, f'rinstance. He used to paint it over with whitewash when Babe objected to pullin' loads over it, so's to make him think it was still snow.

And so it come Paul had his snowshoes and his mackinaw on when he started for the West that mornin', and naturally he didn't take the trouble to take 'em off, but hit right out like he was.

Well, it kept gettin' hotter and hotter, of course, as he went along, and he kept sweatin' and sweatin', and his shoes was gettin' to feel pretty heavy in the dust, but he didn't want to stop for nothin'. He was in a hurry, because he'd like to get in

Seattle for supper that night if he could.

But there was one thing he hadn't figgured on, and that was that his snowshoes would probly warp in the sun. And the south shoe would warp considerable more than the north shoe.

Swingin' his foot out that way with his south shoe warped the most, instead of makin' a straight bee line from Fargo to Seattle the way he intended to, he went around in a great half-circle, so at six o'clock, when he thought he was in Seattle, he found he'd landed up in San Francisco instead, and it was nearly ten o'clock when he finally got into Seattle that night.

On the way he'd dragged his peavey behind him awhile to ease his shoulder some, and that scratch he made with his peavey is now the Grand Canyon. Paul put his peavey back on his shoulder quick when he seen the rut he'd made, but it was too late and the damage was done already, and there's the Grand Canyon, just like you see it, to this day.

Well, there was another outfit loggin' on the Skagit when he got there, sure enough, just like he'd heard reports of.

It was a big outfit, headed by a one-eyed hooktender named Joe Maufree. Joe was six foot and thirty-two inches tall, and had only one eye, on the right side of his nose, and all he could see was saw-logs and choker-hooks. But it wasn't no wonder he hadn't no eye for nothin' else when he didn't have no other eye at all. Big Joe never worked with patent chokers or bull-hooks, they said. When the riggin' slinger would get the logs hooked on the main line, Big Joe just squeezed the hooks together by hand.

Paul heard that Joe had just put in a yardin' engine with 40 inch by 20 inch cylinders, and he knew that was goin' to be pretty stiff competition all right. But of course he didn't worry none. When he'd get Babe out there and really get started, this here Joe wouldn't have a look-in.

"I'll beat 'em, new-fangled methods and all," he says.

But if Paul was goin' to do any loggin' he'd have to get some land first because he didn't have no land claims out here, and he'd have to come by it some way, and the way he done that was by homesteadin', and by scrippin'. He could get a lot of land by scrippin'. Because he could go ahead and scrip some land and then when he'd get all the timber cleared off he could explain that he'd made a mistake and scripped the wrong land and go ahead and scrip some more. That way he could keep right on goin'. And for the homesteadin', he didn't do that himself, of course—he'd get other men to do it for him. He'd get fellers who didn't care much whether they told the truth or not to swear that they was gettin' timber claims for themselves, as homesteaders, and then he'd pay 'em fifty dollars for their deed, and get the land that way. Sometimes— like some of the other timber men did, too—he could get dead men to take up homesteads for him and then he didn't have to pay the fifty dollars.

Well, I was goin' on, though. Paul was goin' to show Joe how to log, and he wasn't goin' to let him get ahead of him, and so, as soon as he got his land staked out, he went back East and got the Blue Ox and other camp equipment. Paul went back to the Ottawa country where he'd left some of his stuff when he'd been loggin' there a long time ago, and then of course the equipment he had to take out of North Dakota, and then a lot of new stuff from Chicago, donkey engines, and cable, and railroad cars, and what-not, and a lot of other new-fangled things he was goin' to use.

"I'll beat 'em at their own game," he says.

And Babe was good for freightin' too. Just as good as for any other kind of woods work.

Start from Montreal in the mornin', dinner at Winnipeg, supper in Vancouver, every day, if Paul wanted to take that many trips, or from Minneapolis to Seattle in an afternoon. And when he'd come to a hill or somethin', Babe would walk right through it—up to his knees in solid rock.

That's the way all them passes through the Cascades was made—Index Pass and the rest of 'em. Index Pass, I know—old John Maloney, who was through there freightin', many times, with Paul and the Ox that time, said he told Jim Hill about it afterwards and so they put the Great Northern railroad through there, but they never compensated Paul for what he'd done, though you'd think they might of.

When Paul and Babe come to a piece of thick woods, Paul generally went ahead of the Ox to make a road for him, where the timber was thick, and it was kind of swampy—like in the Lake of the Woods country. He'd have his ax in his hand—the big one with the sixteen-foot cuttin' surface and the wove grass handle—and he'd swing it back and forth in front of him as he went along and make a road for the Ox. The trees would just fall crosswise across the road as soon as he got past, big end for little end and little end for big end, and make as fine a corduroy as you'd ever want to see, and then the Ox would come along behind.

I used to like to see 'em—Paul comin' through the woods that way slashin' with his ax, with the clean timber road layin' there behind him, and the streak of light showin' through the dark pine trees, and the big Blue Ox comin' along there be-

hind with the load, chewin' his cud as easy and peaceful as if he'd been goin' into his barn in Paul's camp on the Red River.

That's the way Paul done most of his freightin', but sometimes he went farther south across the plains.

One of them times when he was crossin' the plains was when the blacksnake whip was invented.

A snake had caught in a saplin' that Babe was draggin' along stuck in his shoe, and so Paul just stopped and made a whip of it. He cut the snake skin up into several strips so he got a nice long lash to it.

Paul didn't never use that whip on Babe, though. But he'd crack it sometimes just for fun, or make it whistle. If he ever happened to hit a tree, that whip would cut a two-foot log in two, and he got so expert, he could kill a fly on one of Babe's horns when he was standin' a hundred and fifty feet away and never jar the Ox one bit.

I remember one time I was with him on one of those trips when he was bringin' some stuff out, and he had a calf that

he'd bought from some farmer in Iowa that he was bringin'
with him to butcher for his camp on the Skagit, when he'd be
just about the right size then, and so he took him along on this
tote-trip he was makin' across the plains. And after the first
day we stopped over night at a cabin near Billings, Montana.

The young fellow who was homesteadin' there said he'd
put the calf in the barn for the night, so's he'd be protected
from the weather some, and Paul of course was glad at that,
because he knowed that would keep the meat more tender, and
he told him, sure, that would be fine, if he had room enough.

"Well, then I'll do that," says the homesteader.

And so then we put the calf in the barn, and we all put up
for the night.

Well, the next mornin' when we got up and went outside,
somethin' about the place looked kind of funny and we didn't
hardly know at first what it was, but finally one of 'em says:

"I know what's the matter. The barn's gone."

And sure enough when we looked, where it'd been there was
only a pile of straw now, bein' blowed about by the wind.

So then of course we all begun lookin' around to find out
what'd become of it, but we couldn't see it nowheres. It hadn't
been burned, we knowed that, because if it had of there would
of been some ashes, and there wasn't nothin', only just straw
and a few boards of the old floor, just as if it'd been lifted
right up and carried away by the wind. And then we happened to think the calf was in the barn too.

Well, we didn't hardly know what it was could of come
about, and so then Holloway—that's the young fellow homesteadin'—happened to think he had a pair of field glasses
somewheres about the place. For he'd used to a been a forest

ranger before, and so that's how he happened to have the glasses there. Well, he brought 'em out, and we looked around, and finally one of us spied the barn way off in the distance away off towards the south.

"And Gee! it's movin'!" he said.

"No, sure not. There ain't wind enough to be movin' it now. There might of been in the night, but there sure ain't now—no wind at all to speak of."

"But it's movin' just the same. And there's a kind of funny thing on top of it."

Well, we got our saddle ponies and rode on out there and we found the barn, and I'll be blamed if there inside of it wasn't that calf of Paul's.

Or I shouldn't of said inside it, for he was mostly outside.

You know he'd growed so fast in the night he'd grown clean out of it and here was the four sides of the barn hangin' around his legs. He sure was the limit for growin' fast.

The last trip Paul made across the plains when he was bringin' his equipment from North Dakota, Teeny was with him.

She had a bed-tick full of boom chains and dipper teeth to take care of for her dad, and she was sittin' up on a box in the wagon holdin' onto 'em good, but when they come to the Missouri it happened to be floodin' at the time and she floated off.

But Teeny was a good swimmer and she held on tight to the tick full of chains and dipper teeth and swum acrost; she run after her dad and finally caught up with him and the wagon about an hour later over on the Madison.

"Why didn't you wait for me, dad?" she says, and then

Paul looked around and seen her comin' behind the wagon.
And the fact is, he hadn't missed her till then.

"Well, you could of hustled a little bit," he says. "It
wouldn't of hurt you none."

But anyway he was glad she hadn't lost the dipper teeth
and chains, I guess.

Another way Paul had of gettin' his stuff across was by boat,
around the Horn.

He never took that trip himself, though, but sent Red Jack,
his best faller, to take charge of the fleet they'd got together.

They started from Chicago, and got through the Great
Lakes and over the falls and out of the St. Lawrence all right,
and all the way down the Atlantic, but when they got about
near the bottom of South America, they begun havin' bad
luck, and things begun goin' against them.

For one thing a storm had just come off the Horn, and for
another Jack had just broke the rudder on his main ship.

Well, the waves big the way they was, Jack couldn't steer
acrost them because his rudder was broke, and he got down
between two of 'em and got swamped first thing.

And then the other ships, that'd got so used to followin',
all followed the flagship, naturally, and so then here they all
was, down in the holler of the wave with the water pourin'
down over 'em on all sides.

And so then there wasn't nothin' could be done about it,
and they was all drowned.

But Jack, when he seen how the water was pourin' in, and
that there wasn't no way of gettin' his ship out, he crawled
out of the holler himself and up on top of the next wave and
so he saved his own life that way. And then he happened to

HE CRAWLED OUT OF THE HOLLER HIMSELF

think he had a shipment of crowbars on one of the ships and he went back and got some of 'em, and made himself a raft, and so finally he got to land.

He had a few ships' biscuits in his pocket and so he didn't starve to death and he steamed into Seattle a few weeks later with his flag a-wavin'—which was his blue handkerchief from around his neck, that he'd put up for a flag—and he said he hadn't met up with no more bad weather. Most of it is just hangin' round the Horn there anyway, he said, and don't generally get no further.

Paul just happened to be comin' in from one of his overland trips East when Red Jack arrived, and naturally he was surprised to see him—alone that way, and without no ships.

"Where did you come from?" he says to him. "And what did you do with them ships of mine?"

And then Red Jack begun to tell him about the storm and how he'd left all the ships down between two waves just off the Horn, and then how he'd salvaged the crowbars and floated home on 'em.

Well, Paul, of course, was mighty glad to have Red Jack back safe, but he was sorry about the cargo they'd lost and about all the men that had got drowned—said he'd never knowed about the Horn that it blowed so hard.

One thing they'd lost down there was the big hotcake griddle.

Jack said last he seen of it, it was standin' right straight up just south of the Horn, dividin' the Pacific and Atlantic oceans. It wasn't so bad, he figgured, to've lost her right there, because the oceans need somethin' like that to keep 'em apart now that they was goin' to be connected by the Panama Canal and might get mixed up together.

Of course Paul had to get somethin' else in place of a griddle for his camp on the Skagit, to fry hotcakes on, but he'd kind of figgured to get somethin' else anyway, for he wanted everythin' in that new camp to be new and up-to-date, so's he could show Joe what was the proper way of loggin'.

And so he said when he went back to Minneapolis for his mail the next Saturday night he'd look around a bit and see if there wasn't somethin' else he could find to use in place of the griddle.

NEW METHODS

FTER Paul'd finished movin' the Ox and his other equipment, he set up his new camp out here in the Northwest, and it was some camp, let me tell you—the finest and biggest he'd ever had. If you ever liked to see loggin' that was loggin' and a camp outfit that was a camp outfit, you should of seen that camp of Paul's that he set up on the Coast here. He'd said he was goin' to show that hooktender, Joe, and he certainly showed him all right.

The kitchens in Paul's new camp was so big that you couldn't see hardly from one end to the other when the steam was thick, and the donkey engines he had here was so big every time the bull-wheel turned around it was pay-day.

Oh, it took Paul some time to get all his camp equipment hauled out here, but when he finally got it all together, I'll tell you the camp he set up was somethin' nothin' in the whole world could be compared with.

The cook-range in Paul's new cook-house was of blue steel and was twenty-four blocks long. That was what Paul'd made up his mind to have instead of the old hotcake griddle. It was so slick the cook didn't never have to put grease on it to fry hotcakes with. They'd just slide on and slide off just about automatically, as you might say, and they'd get up such a speed when they come off the stove they'd keep on goin' right on down through the air-shafts and out onto the plates where they was to be ate by the men. The flunkies had new roller-skates provided 'em every mornin' to skate on, and the head cook, surrounded by four hundred cooks and six hundred flunkies, rode up and down in front of the stove on a motor-cycle shoutin' his orders through a megaphone with patent amplifiers. The tables down the dinin' room was so long that when the waiters was sent down to the lower end for some-thin', they hardly ever come back. Sometimes their grand-children did, though, and then some of 'em would happen to be girls, and then, naturally, there was trouble.

There was a car-track down the middle of the table, so part of the food could be sent down by express, but you had to grab fast if you was goin' to get any of it, for the trains didn't hardly ever run slower than eighty-five miles an hour, and so it would be all gone before it got in front of you.

Pipes and sprinklers up in the ceilin' was turned on after each meal to wash off the tables, and pipe lines also led to the ketchup and vinegar bottles. It always took one man to keep the valves turned on and off, and he'd generally get around to all of 'em about once in three days.

Of course a good deal of the food, like the beans and pea-soup, come in through tubes in the roof by long distance, like I guess I mentioned before. The range was given to the gunners at the main gun every mornin' and they'd shoot the carloads of beans and bacon out to the kitchen, one carload of bacon and five ton of beans to each shot. The bacon was always shot first and that greased the air for the beans to follow, and both was cooked thorough by the friction they made on the way.

In the kitchens the cooks was all dressed in white uniforms and the flunkies was in blue pants and white coats, and they had all the conveniences to work with always—pie-dough stretchers, dish-washin' eliminatin' machines, cake mixers and frosters, biscuit raisers, hotcake slides, and a 60-foot band saw to cut the eight ton of bread that was used each meal, and four 10-block shingle machines for slicin' and peelin' potatoes.

The bunkhouse was built like a hotel and was so high that the last seven stories had to be put on hinges to let the moon go by—Paul didn't have only 14,000 men at this camp, because it was his headquarters, and he never liked to have a crowd around. Each logger had a room individually by himself with a shower-bath and wash-dish, and the spittoons in the reception room was all polished brass. It was kind of hard, of course, for the men to get used to 'em, after you'd learned to hit in the middle of the acorn on the side of the stove, the way we used to in the old camps.

And Paul's woods equipment was like his kitchens and his bunkhouse—on a scale a good deal similar—bigger and better than he'd ever had before. He got a yardin' engine that was so big, the Japs he had workin' for him used to get in the

injector and get sucked up in the water-glass and we'd have a
hard time gettin' 'em out. And the cylinder was so long, a man
could walk inside it for four days and not get to the end.
Course the reason Paul got it was, he wanted to show Joe.
Though there wasn't really no sense to it—Joe couldn't no
more compete with Paul than nothin', though he did try a
little at first.

One time, I know, in the spring, Joe imported an ostrich
from California and challenged Paul to a race with the
Blue Ox.

Paul hadn't never gone in for racin', and wasn't at all
anxious to go, but he kind of pretty near had to, the way
Joe put it, to save Babe's reputation, so he said finally, go
ahead, he'd race him.

The day they picked out for the race was the 4th of July,
and the track was laid out as close to the 49th parallel as they
could without interferin' with the boundry, from a line
drawed six miles west of Winnipeg to a point in South Bellingham where the big hotel stands.

The parallel was lined on both sides with loggers, and over
forty-three million dollars changed hands in bets that day.

First the bettin' was pretty strong on the ostrich, but that
changed, naturally, as soon as Paul's men got to bettin', and
by the time the race was goin' to be pulled off they was goin'
straight 16 to 1 on Babe, and they'd take up anyone that
wanted to put up.

"Sixteen to one on Babe! Sixteen to one on the Ox!" they
was yellin' all along the line.

Paul Bunyan's men was all loyal to Babe, of course, and
they knowed he was goin' to win, too. It wasn't that he was

HE WAS A KIND OF A NERVOUS BIRD

so swift, but he was so big that even goin' slow, or just standin' still even, he covered a good deal of ground, and they didn't think no ostrich was ever goin' to get ahead of him.

Paul had Babe's horns tipped with brass for the occasion, and it took nearly four ton of brass to do it, Ole said. He'd had the hair along the top of his back trimmed off a little and had kept him away strictly from hotcakes for a week, and he had a red, white, and blue flag stuck up on a long pole standin' up on his tail, with a Union Jack flyin' at half mast. Nobody'd ever seen Babe look so gay before, but I believe the extra weight, and the fol-de-rols, and all, sort of bothered him. Anyway that's the way he acted. They couldn't hardly get him in line at all, or get him to start when he should of.

And so the ostrich was a little ahead at first. He was kind of a nervous bird and got a false start, and Buffalo Bill, who acted as starter, didn't make him go back and do it over again.

I suppose the ostrich must of been about eight miles off before Babe even lifted a foot.

But when he did, though, there wasn't much to it. The ostrich was left lopin' miles behind in no time, and Babe arrived at the corner in South Bellingham, amid the cheerin', six hours before his shadow.

They found out afterwards the ostrich had lost his breath tryin' to keep up at first, and it took a couple of camp inspectors pretty near a whole month to find it for him.

That was the only race Babe ever was in, that I know of, but Paul had him at a County Fair once to show how he could pull a tree out without takin' the bark and limbs with it, but leave them still standin' on the stump.

The brass tips on the horns he always kept on afterwards,

for trimmin' for Babe. They'd shine pretty out in the woods when the sun come in through the tops of the trees around noon—like it did occasionally, even in them woods.

Paul had to change a good many of his methods, loggin' in the West, from what he'd been used to use back in Michigan and Dakota, where the winters had been long and cold and sometimes there was a year with two winters even, when it was winter all summer; and out here it wasn't so easy for him to get ice for his ice-roads like it had been. That was one of the worst things Paul had to meet up with when he come out here to the Coast. He tried to make some in his ice-plant, but he'd no sooner get it run out on the roads than the rain would come and melt it.

So then what he done was, he just built a railroad north and south and pulled the logs in from both sides with high-lead loggin', and didn't try to use ice-roads no more the way he'd always done before.

The engines that Paul used on this railroad was so big that the boilers had to be made in sections so's they could go round the curves, and the smokestacks couldn't never be made of anythin' but tarpaper, because if they was, they'd be so heavy they'd sink through and into the ground, and stop the speed of the engine.

Afterwards, when he extended this railroad down into Mexico, the Mexicans used to beat their way to Alaska by gettin' into the oilcups, and hidin' there on the way up. And the headlights on the locomotives on this railroad was so big they was pretty near strong enough to shine through an Everett fog, but not quite.

Paul built a shingle mill too, along with his camp on the

Coast, so as to make use of the short logs and stumps, the cedar ones, especially. He had fourteen hundred filers for this mill and he had nine miles of uprights and at the beginnin' he did all the packin' himself.

There was just one packin' frame and bin and the shingles was carried to this bin in conveyors. Paul was such a fast packer that it took two men to oil his frames and one to pour ice-water on his packin' hammer to keep it cool, and even then it burnt up and Paul had to quit and let some of the other men go on with the job.

Paul was branchin' out in all kinds of new lines, and he built a saw-mill too, though he had kind of bad luck with that at first.

You know, the way that was, he ordered all the parts from the East, knocked down, and then he hired an Englishman to put it together for him.

Well, that Englishman was like most of 'em—contrary. Of course if Paul had knowed it was an Englishman he wouldn't of hired him, but he didn't know that, and so he give him the contract and let him go ahead.

Well, when it was done, and Paul come to inspect it, he thought it looked kind of funny and he tried to tell Jamison so. But, of course, bein' an Englishman, he just got up on his high horse and said he refused to talk about it.

"I have arranged all the parts as per specifications," he says, or something like that.

And so then they went ahead and set up the mill the way it was.

Well, I always knowed Englishmen was contrary, but I never knowed how contrary they could be, till that time.

Come to find out, here if that fellow hadn't set up every part of that saw-mill wrong end to, so when we hooked the motor on it and started it runnin', it begun runnin' backwards, turnin' out saw logs instead of lumber, and wouldn't take nothin' but sawdust for feed.

And so then Paul had to take it all apart again and put it together himself.

And of course that Englishman never saw the joke. Couldn't expect him to, though, for that matter, they never do.

I don't know that I mentioned before, the planin'-mill that Paul had connected up with this saw-mill, was so big that the men could never keep their hats on, but what they was always flyin' away and gettin' lost up in the blower, till they got some strings on 'em and tied 'em under their chins and so kept their hats on that way.

Oh, there was some inconveniences and some things that wasn't so comfortable in this new-style loggin' too. I can't say as I liked that new-fangled camp of Paul's myself so very much, and there was some of the oldtimers that just balked and wouldn't take to it at all.

Old Mack Stiles, I know, who'd worked for Paul for forty-five years straight. And Gus Peterson, a friend of his.

They wouldn't go into the new bunkhouse at all, on no account, but went and built themselves a shack over on the other side of the tracks instead, where they could have it the way they wanted it. And not have to sleep between sheets and wash in marble wash troughs, and spit in brass spittoons, but could be comfortable like in the old days. Some of us used to go in and visit 'em sometimes, and it seemed kind of nice, too.

It was even kind of hard on a few of the real oldtimers, who'd followed loggin' all their lives and hadn't never been out of the woods. Some of 'em even died. One took pneumonia from takin' a bath and then changin' his shirt right afterwards. It was only February, and he hadn't never changed it that early before.

But most of us, myself included, naturally didn't have no objections to the decenter livin' quarters, and the better conveniences, and all that. It wasn't that so much, but it was the old-time spirit that was gone now, that we objected to.

You couldn't get any of the old-time life and fun back into the men any more, it looked like. Steam heat ain't conducive to it. It took the old comboose and the deacon-seat we used to have, to really bring it out of 'em.

Them days the men all knowed each other. Used to come back to the same camp year after year and when they come in the fall they generally stayed all winter, most of 'em anyway, especially the Michigan men. Wisconsin quitters, Minnesota kickers, Michigan stickers, they used to say.

And that way we'd sit around the fire in the winter and spin yarns and sing some of them fine old shanty songs, or maybe listen to one of the men fiddlin'. We had some fine fiddlers in camp sometimes, and we used to have some real music.

But now it ain't that way no more. Now in the camps the men just jump around from one camp to another and don't never stay in the same place very long. And there's all kinds of 'em. Japs and Hawaiians and Hindoos and Polacks and Bulgarians and I don't know what all, and you never know any of 'em.

And all they ever think about is to get to town on Saturday

night, and get away, get away all the time. And when you do meet one you want to talk to, all they want to talk about is politics or capital and labor or economics or something like that, or else somethin' they read in the Argonaut or Windy Stories or the Literary Digest. Oh, I ain't sayin' it ain't all right. I wouldn't argue with anybody on that. I know they've done a lot of good in bringin' about better workin' conditions and shorter workin' hours and a lot of things like that that we wouldn't of had without them agitators, but a man who's known the old days, when he goes into a camp, misses the fine old spirit we used to have, and can't help but notice the restlessness around him.

Them used to be fine old days, the old days—and I guess any old logger would agree with me—even if we did have to work from two hours before daylight till two hours after dark then, and sleep in spruce bough bunks and carry our own roll of blankets.

THE INLAND EMPIRE

OME of the finest loggin' Paul done after he come West was in the Inland Empire. Course it wasn't an Inland Empire then but just a big inland sea, and it was around the shores of this lake and on an island in the northwest corner of it that Paul Bunyan logged. It was pretty near my favorite loggin' with Paul, that year was. The location was mighty fine, for one thing.

The island was covered all over with Sequoia trees—the biggest trees you ever saw—so tall the tops pretty near touched the sky. They took on some of the color from the sky and was blue about half way down their branches, and then below that they was green, with brown trunks. And the ground was all covered with brown needles, pretty near two feet long, and layin' in figgurs, just like the way they had fallen, circles and figgurs with kind of points to 'em just like the branches are arranged on the trees. And them tall ferns growin' in places and sometimes the sunlight comin' through and lightin' 'em up in spots, so parts of 'em shine all light green just like they do when they first come out in the spring, and the whole air between the trees, even where the dark shade is, full of that green and white light. It sure is pretty.

And the old logs layin' on the ground with moss four inches thick, and young, branchy salal bushes and green vines growin' all over 'em.

And everything so quiet the only thing you can hear is your own steps as you walk along, or some little animal skootin' under a log and cracklin' the twigs or dead ferns, or the trickle of water from a little stream comin' out of a rock wall alongside of you, and makin' a little pool at the bottom and a muddy place across the trail.

And then of course, besides bein' pretty, it was good loggin' down there, too, with them big trees like that.

I know when we first come down there Paul went out to cut a tree down one day. He cut away for a couple of hours, and then he went round to see how much he had left to chop before he'd get through, and here if he didn't find two Irishmen choppin' away on the other side of the tree and they'd been choppin' there for over three years, they said, ever since the spring of the Long Rain just about three years before that. It seems some boss had sent 'em in there to cut that tree down and that's all the farther they'd got, and I suppose the boss had forgot all about 'em a long time ago.

They was all overgrown with beards and they was lean and hungry of course, and kind of wild too and queer from havin' been away from civilization so long and not havin' seen nobody for such a long time.

Paul felt mighty sorry for 'em and so he said he'd see what he could do, and he went back to his own side again and got his other ax and chopped away a little faster, because the men was starvin' to death, and between 'em in an hour or so they got it down.

And then I'll be blamed after all that trouble if the old tree wasn't hollow.

But generally they was pretty sound and in good shape and Paul could figgur on a lot of timber in 'em.

One Sunday down there he went out with a cruisin' party and the rest of the company with the packhorses was up ahead and Paul was a little behind the others figgurin' on some trees just then—he generally always wore a mill-scale around on his spectacles so's he could figgur 'em up as he went along—and the men that was up ahead come to a river and couldn't get acrost it, and when Paul come up to them, here they all was standin' on the bank and wonderin' how they was ever goin' to get acrost that river, for it was a deep and wide one comin' down off the big glacier on top of Mt. Pasco.

But Paul wasn't stumped for more'n a minute or two. What he done was, he just fell one of them there big trees over the river, and then when he'd got it down and split it open, he let the two sides fall apart, and there you had a bridge wide enough so you could of taken an army acrost it, if you'd wanted to. And so that way he never had to bother with bridges there.

About a couple of months after that Paul was walkin' along in the woods one day and he had the Blue Ox along, leadin' him on a rope, and he was lettin' him wander around some, grazin' on the salal bushes and some of the young pine growth, because it was kind of hard to find feed for him that he liked there on the island.

Well, they was gettin' along all right and had walked quite a few miles when Babe seen an especially green bunch of young spruce trees on the other side of a big brush pile where they'd been fallin' trees, and naturally, like they say, the fodder on the other side of the brush pile always looks the greenest, and Babe was stretchin' his neck in that direction and was just bound he was goin' over and get some of it. Well, Paul figgured around a little bit and then he thought it wouldn't be no harm to let him go, he could easy find him a little further on along the trail, and he wouldn't get lost, he guessed, and if he did he'd probly find his way back to camp all right. And so he let go of the rope and let Babe go where he pleased, and Paul kept on on the way to camp, figgurin' up the timber both sides of the trail as he went along.

But when the dinnerhorn tooted that night there wasn't no Babe to be seen, and next mornin' even he hadn't showed up yet.

And Paul hunted for three whole days for that Ox and pretty near the whole camp was out huntin' for him. We didn't get nothin' else done all that time, but the swampers, and the sawyers, and we buckers, and all of 'em was layin' off to help in that hunt, even half of the bull-cooks and flunkies, though they should really of kept on the job. And we just combed that island from one side to the other, but no sir, no Babe could be found.

And so Paul was just about goin' to give up the hunt, thinkin' that spirits must of took him away, or one of them big sea birds, when he happened to be walkin' along in the woods that day feelin' pretty blue and he heard a kind of little funny noise inside the limb of one of them there old trees layin' on the ground, and he begun to figgur what in the world it could be in there. Well, he went into camp and got a couple of the sawyers, and they come out there and sawed the limb off, and I'll be blamed if there wasn't Babe, and Paul sure was glad to see him.

And Babe was pretty glad to see Paul, too. Poor fellow! we didn't hardly know where all he'd been wanderin' around all that time. Must of gone from one limb to another and found 'em all blind alleys, poor old fellow. Charley Granger looked around and found the hole in one of the limbs where he must of got in and an end of the rope where he had wore it off in there, and followed it along and found it tangled up in all kinds of places where Babe'd been walkin', lookin' for a place to get out.

And as luck would have it, just like it always happens in them cases, he'd just missed the main trunk by a hair's breadth. There was a kind of knot stickin' out just in front of the openin' into the main trunk, and Babe'd followed partly around that knot, like Charley said he could tell by the way the rope laid afterwards, and then must of walked off into the lowest limb on the right and then into the next one where Paul found him.

Must of had a pretty black, dark time of it. He was so glad when he got out he frisked around, and jumped, and waved his tail so there got to be a pretty considerable breeze all over there in the treetops, and Paul give him some hotcakes and then he was the same old Babe, but we noticed he was always a little shy in the woods after that.

They organized an explorin' party to explore the trunk of that tree and after about four weeks they come out and built up a fire for a signal fire to show they had arrived in daylight again, and Paul and some of the rest of us took some grub for 'em and went out there, but then, I tell you, Paul was mad, and I don't blame him. For it was just the same tree he'd chopped so long on the time he found the Irishmen, and here it was givin' him more trouble again. The Irishmen recognized it by the year lines where it showed how far they'd chopped each year.

Them Irishmen was still in camp, for Paul had fed 'em up and made 'em look right and told 'em they could stay and work for him if they wanted to, and so of course naturally they'd stayed. Nobody didn't want to work for no other loggin' boss if he got a chance to work for Paul Bunyan, especially down there on that island.

Loggin' on the island and around the inland sea was sure mighty handy. For one thing, there wasn't no waste. You could cut up the main part of the tree into them special lengths Paul was gettin' out that year, and then you could cut up all the limbs into just ordinary size logs and that way there wasn't no waste at all. And all them small logs filled up the spaces between the big ones and made a nice solid-lookin' job of it.

The way Paul done, he just cut the trees around the edge of the island first—the first row of 'em all around—and fell them right out into the lake where they'd be all ready for the drive, and filled in on top with them smaller logs, and then the next row of trees on top of the first ones, and the next row on top of that, and so on, one circle layin' right inside and at the same time kind of on top of the next circle, till the whole island

PAUL . . . PLOWED OUT AN OUTLET FOR IT

was one solid pile of logs, way till you got to the center, to the mountain. Mt. Pasco was right up in the middle of the island and that's where we had the camp of course. Not a very high mountain but kind of big and flat, with a crater in the top of it, and a hollow where you could cook the soup always by natural heat.

And then the trees from the sides of the lake he cut out in the water too, but we finished up the island first. From the south shore of the lake when you got away from it far enough the island used to look like a great big hotcake layin' out there, all nice and brown, and kind of high in the middle like it had plenty of good egg and soda in it, and then kind of a little uneven around the edge like a good hotcake always ought to be.

It was sure as pretty a raft of logs as you'd ever want to see, and the biggest one I ever knowed of Paul havin'. The sunshine was mighty bright there in the inland empire and used to lay over them brown logs out there so you could almost see the air movin' in heat waves above them, even though everything else was still, and out over the blue sea too, till you couldn't hardly look at it, it was so bright. Loggin' there was different from most of the loggin' we'd done, and we liked it.

And then when we got the raft all ready and everythin' layin' just the way we wanted it Paul went down to the southwest corner of the lake and plowed out an outlet for it. He was goin' to take most of them logs to China, so he figgered from that corner would be the best way to get out to the ocean. And then when he got the river finished and about half filled up with water and slicked out over the top so it would be slippery he turned the lake right into it.

Runnin' out so fast there, of course, the inland sea right

away begun to slant from the northeast to the southwest, and
the whole hotcake of logs just slid right off the island and
floated right down to the outlet and then pretty soon the logs
from the sides begun to slide in after it trailin' along behind,
till goin' down the river it looked like a great big sea turtle
with its hair streamin' out behind it. And it wasn't long till
it was gone and clean out of sight. And so that loggin' was
over.

We was all mighty surprised to find that that lake wasn't
near as deep as we'd thought it might be, but real shallow, and
it wasn't more'n a couple hours after the raft had gone by, till
it was all drained out and dry and the sagebrush had begun
to grow up all over it. The sunshine still lays over it, bright
and in kind of waves like it did before, and that's the way you
see it today, a fine beautiful country, stretchin' out far and
wide to the East and West, or rather I should say to the Northeast and the Southwest, and full of sagebrush and sunshine.

But the Inland Empire is pretty nice at that, though, if you
like that kind of country. It's a fine wheat country, and pretty
good for fruit, too, and I guess the people there ain't sorry
Paul Bunyan logged it off for 'em.

ON THE COLUMBIA

HERE'S many conflictin' stories about how Paul dug the Columbia River, but of course there's only one right one and that's the one I was just tellin' about the Inland Empire. I was right there and I saw how it was done. When Paul got his raft of logs finished and was ready to take 'em out he just went out there and plowed out the river. And there wasn't nothin' to it at all. He plowed it out first and then filled it up with water and evened it out so it would be nice and smooth for his logs to slide over. On a windy day in the Gorge when an east wind is blowin' you can see the hole yet in the water where Paul never put in the last bucketful when he was evenin' it out.

But some of them other stories is interestin' just to show how such stories grow up.

I know there's some that says it happened just by accident.

Paul was havin' Babe pull a big log chain into a solid bar that he wanted, and the bar broke before it was finished, and Babe'd got such a start he couldn't stop, but run all the way to Astoria pullin' the piece of chain behind him. It cut up quite a scratch as it went along, and that scratch, they say, is the Columbia River.

I was in a little hotel up at Acme once, settin' at a table with some other loggers, and one of them settin' at the end eatin' pie, started in to tell how Paul dug the Columbia purposely, and how he used tamed mountain goats to do the work with. Proof of that is that there ain't no mountain goats south of the river now. Just at the time the water was turned in the teams of goats all happened to be workin' on the north side and that's why they haven't never got across.

It was partikkelarly interestin' to me, of course, because that fellow had the nerve to say that he was on that job—Paul had him to trim the beards on his goats to keep 'em from gettin' all galled up. The beards used to grow long and get under the breast strap on the harness and rub until there was a sore there and then the goats wouldn't pull good.

Anyway, no matter what they say about it, the Columbia is a fine river to have a highway alongside of, the way they've got down there.

When he was loggin' in Oregon Paul built up Mt. Hood for a kind of lookout place, from where to watch his different camps; for he had a lot of foreigners workin' for him that year and they wouldn't work without somebody havin' to watch 'em all the time. Paul hired a kind of efficiency expert to help him on that, and that fellow, Gerber, used to walk around among the different camps and keep tab on the men and count up how they spent their time, and he certainly could make up some big figgurs, all right.

He always put down whenever anybody stopped to borrow a chew, and how long it took him, and counted up how long it took the men to light their pipes, or ask the time of day, or go for a drink, and kept tab on how much time was spent in talkin' baseball, or dodgin' the straw boss, or gettin' ready for quittin' time, and it always added up to a pretty considerable figgur, especially that last item. He used to try to make his accounts balance up with the time in the timekeeper's book, but he couldn't quite make that, though.

It was a hard job he had, all right, and he had to keep steppin' all the time.

He tried to increase his efficiency one time by swallowin' a watch and so makin' himself work automatic, but that didn't work out good, because the mainspring broke inside him and busted him.

The first watch he had, Paul had imported for him from Connecticut.

It was such a good watch it gained enough time in the first three days to pretty near pay for itself.

But when he bragged about it to Paul, Paul said he guessed he'd have to sell it. At that rate, he says, it might be Doomsday before he'd get his loggin' in Oregon done. And so Paul sold the watch afterwards to a fellow down in New Mexico. On account of the earth bein' bigger down there the watch wouldn't be able to gain so fast.

Paul made a good deal of lumber down in Oregon and most of it he shipped to Japan. He had a band saw in his mill and three different cutting floors, and a carriage on each one. The top band wheel was in the roof and the bottom one below the first floor. But when they started this mill runnin' the sawyer on the bottom begun kickin' because he was cuttin' with a dull saw all the time, and so then Paul punched teeth on the back side of the saw and pointed 'em upward and then ran the mill backwards every other day and that way they cut a lot of lumber, and everybody was satisfied.

Paul built one of the biggest steamships that was ever seen, to take his lumber to Japan. All the old steamboat men remember her. I know she had forty-two decks and not a single bottom and her boilers was all of rubber.

The way that happened, Paul wanted to load her mighty heavy and at the same time he wanted to make a great speed, and the engineer says to him:

"I can't go at any such rate as that," he says. "The boilers would bust if I tried to get up a pressure for a speed like that."

"Well, I tell you," says Paul, "make 'em of rubber then. That way they'll give, when we want 'em to, and then we can go just as fast as we've a mind to."

And so they made 'em of rubber, and they never had no accident with 'em. But of course the smokestack had to be awful big. I know one time Paul sent a man up to paint it, and a long time afterwards the man's grandson come down and asked if he could have some more paint.

Paul kept this lumber ship of his as long as he was loggin' in Oregon, but then he sold her. She was sunk afterwards, and the remainder of her is now called Catalina Island. The Wrigley Chewin' Gum Company salvaged the rubber boilers, and they're usin' some of the material yet for makin' their chewin' gum.

Paul liked Oregon all right, but one thing he sure didn't like and that was the fog. And it made him lose money too —the time they shingled the cook-shanty, f'rinstance, they shingled forty foot out on the fog before they noticed it, and there was all them perfectly good cedar shingles gone to waste, for when the fog lifted it was so thick it just took that part of the roof up with it.

Some of the people down in Oregon was always wantin'

Paul to make somethin' for 'em, some place where tourists could go to spend their money before goin' to California, and they was after him all the time. And so finally he said he'd make Crater Lake for 'em—some of 'em had been sayin' they thought a lake like that would be nice—and he said, all right, he'd go ahead with it.

The snow left from the Winter of the Blue Snow was still layin' about fifty foot thick up on the tops of the Cascades and Paul went up with Babe to bring it down to make a lake of.

Babe got lost a number of times on the way up, by fallin' into drifts, and it made it hard to find him, because he was just about exactly the same color as the snow. And another thing was, his hoofprints was so heavy—weighed pretty near a ton each—and if he got lost they was always so far apart it was a hard thing to carry 'em up and get the connection between 'em.

But Paul and Babe finally got there though, and Paul used a big scraper to haul out the snow, and he dumped all the loads in Crater Lake. Each load was 196 cubic tons, and there was 465 loads in all.

The snow meltin' in the lake the next summer made it blue, and it made it awful wintry cold too, at the same time, like it is. But it's a mighty pretty lake, though.

In fact the only job I ever knowed of Paul doin' that wasn't just up to snuff was the Palouse job, and that's one of them he done while he was loggin' in Oregon, too. He shouldn't of tackled it in the first place if he couldn't do it right, I always said.

The way it was: Old man Palouse hired him to come over and clear the Palouse country for him, and so then Paul went

HE DUMPED ALL THE LOADS IN CRATER LAKE

over there and logged it off and cleared the stumps out and scraped it up. But he had somethin' else on his mind all the time—another job he wanted to do—and so he didn't do a good job of it and never leveled it out smooth afterwards, the way he should of. Babe never liked that part of the work anyway. Always hated to lay on his side so long while Paul hauled him around to even out the bumps.

So Paul got in a hurry and wanted to get away from there, and so what he done was, he just got a couple of quarts of sagebrush whisky and went up to see old man Palouse, and gave him a drink or two, and then in the mornin' he took the old man up to the top of a high hill and showed him the country. Old man Palouse was pretty much gone from the drinks he'd had and anyway from where they was standin' the country looked real level and nice, so Paul got him to accept the contract and call it finished. And Paul tore away like a hurricane to his next job. He never could wait when he had a new job in sight, and so that's why the Palouse country is so hilly and rough like it is. Paul was always ashamed of himself for it, and they say he wept the Great Salt Lake full of tears because he was sorry, but I don't believe that. He made the lake, partly anyhow, to have salt on hand for Babe.

The job that Paul was goin' to when he left the Palouse country was one he'd invented himself, and took a notion of— not really new, of course, because it was somethin' the same as he'd done the time of the Underground Railroad.

He dug the Underground Railroad and let 'em use it for a time while they needed it, and then, afterwards, he made it over for the Standard Oil Company. The tube wasn't just in the right place and was a little too thick for a pipe-line, so he pulled it out long, and stretched it out all the way down to their oil fields in Texas for the Standard Oil people, and they was very well satisfied with the job he made of it.

The idea he had down in Oregon was, there was a good many holes in different parts of the state—prospectors' holes, where they'd been diggin' for gold, and oil wells they'd dug that hadn't never given no oil—and Paul thought if you could get all them holes together they'd be good to use for post-holes when the pioneers and farmers would come along afterwards. He could sell 'em at a profit maybe, or he might give 'em away to them that was needin' 'em. Anyway it was a shame to let 'em all go to waste.

So Paul took Babe, and they went out through the country and pulled up holes. It was light, easy work, because the holes didn't weigh much to speak of, and then Paul tied 'em all together in a string and took 'em to a mountain side to cache 'em —just made a hole in the mountain and pulled 'em through pretty near over to the other side, and then plugged up the hole.

And after he'd got it done he didn't think no more about it, but just went away and left 'em there.

Well, I don't know if Paul ever went back to look for them post-holes or not, or if he ever means to go back again and try to locate 'em. Anyway, he wasn't there when they was found.

For when the Union Pacific was puttin' their railroad through there, the engineers was makin' surveys and, without knowin' it, they started in to put their tunnel right in the identical spot where Paul had hid all the holes.

The chief engineer set a gang of men to work diggin', and then he went away to tend to some other work, and the very first pick that was put in the mountain, they struck the holes, and the air that was in there started to come out. The heat of the friction from havin' been crowded in there so close blowed the whole crew of men off to nowheres so's they was never seen again. Just a little boy who they had for water carrier was left. He told the chief engineer what had happened, and the engineer seen the tunnel was all through and finished up in fine shape. So he didn't have to use no crew of men to dig the tunnel, but he collected for full time from the railroad company just the same—same as if he'd had a full company workin' all the time.

One time Paul'd went in for a little minin' himself.

The claim Paul staked out—and now I got to be careful, for minin' ain't in my line neither no more than it was Paul's —was from an old stump that was a landmark in that part of the country where he was then, just due southwest of where Mars cuts the Milky Way, then north 80 chains, 3 links and a swivel, then east 40 paces stepped off with the Blue Ox to a blue spot in the sky, then proceedin' South 38 chains 4 links, thence southwest to the stump where was the place of beginnin'—Paul'd had a lawyer help him make it out in the first place. It was a gold mine, and it had started out to be a placer deposit but had changed its mind afterwards. But of course on the outside it looked the same as it had always done.

Paul worked the mine for two months, he doin' all the work and furnishin' the provisions, and the lawyer sellin' the stock and collectin' the money. Paul said that lawyer wanted to borrow the Blue Ox, too, so's he could water the stock, but Paul drawed the line on that.

After workin' for a while, Paul took a little of the gravel

to an assayer's office to have it tested—and now let me see if I can remember the right words for that. It was—igneous—prehistoric—and erroneous, that's what it was. Paul's mine was reported to be igneous, prehistoric, and erroneous.

And that was the first and last of Paul's minin' experiments, for he was sure plum disgusted. And from there he went back to his loggin' again, up near Astoria.

DIGGING
PUGET SOUND

HAT year Paul was loggin' down at Astoria and he was just finishin' up his work there the next summer when one Saturday night he lost a couple of rafts of logs on the Columbia River bar; and that was about the time Mr. Rainier come down to see him, about the first part of August that year. Paul'd knowed Mr. Rainier when he first come out West at the time he was gettin' ready to scrip his land that he had to have, but he'd just about forgot all about him. But I guess Mr. Rainier thought the acquaintance was strong enough for him to ask a favor of Paul and anyway that's what he come down to see him for.

Paul went up and got out a raft of logs first and got it down in the river to take the place of the ones he'd lost on Saturday, and then he come in and sat down and started in to talk to Mr. Rainier, who'd been sittin' there in the office waitin' for him most of the afternoon. But Paul thought it was kind of funny, I guess, for he wasn't used to havin' any visitors come to see him that way. But anyway they talked about the weather for a couple of hours, and then about old times what they could remember, and then they didn't have nothin' more to talk about for a while, and so finally Mr. Rainier come out with what he wanted.

"And so we'd like to have you come up and help us dig the Sound," he says.

And Paul says: "I guess I can do that. Loggin's kind of slow anyway this time of the year. Though it ain't hardly in my line," he says.

The way that was: Mr. Rainier and Mr. Puget of the Puget Construction Company, and Old Dad Hood and Mr. Elliott was associated together under a contract to dig a Sound for Seattle so's Seattle would have a harbor, and they'd been given just two years by the goverment to finish the job, and now already twenty-two months was up and they seen they wasn't goin' to get it done, and so that's why they sent down for Paul to come and help 'em. The Republicans in Congress was askin' the contractors to report progress and the contractors naturally didn't have no progress to report and they figgured they'd have to hurry up and do somethin' about it, and I guess they was pretty near up a stump.

"We ain't gettin' this Sound dug," says Old Man Puget.

"No, we ain't," says Dad Hood.

"Except of course I pretty near got the Bay dug though, with my badgers and catapults," says Mr. Elliott.

"The bay ain't half finished," says Old Man Puget, "and besides what good's a bay goin' to do without a Sound behind

it, I'd like to know. We got to do somethin' different than
that, I reckon."

And so then Mr. Rainier suggested havin' met Paul Bunyan one time and the Blue Ox, and Old Man Puget says, "As
chairman, that's just the point I was comin' to."

And so then he made his proposition in the legal and proper
form.

What they proposed to do was that they should send down
for Paul to come up and dig the Sound for 'em and they'd give
him part of the money that they was goin' to get, because
they'd have to, but keep a good big margin for themselves,
because they was the ones that was lettin' the contract and so
was entitled to it. And they didn't need to say anythin' to him
about the mountain they was goin' to make of course.

When they'd took the contract to dig the Sound they
knowed they was goin' to have to have some place to dump the
dirt, and so they'd got their Congressman from Seattle to in-
troduce a bill in Congress that they should make somethin' for
Tacoma too at the same time and a mountain would be just
the thing, that they could name after their city. And so that
way the contractors could get paid twice for doin' the one job
of course. But now they wouldn't have to say nothin' to Paul
about that, but could just tell him where to dump the dirt.

And so then they sent Mr. Rainier, the secretary, down to
see Paul about it, and like I said, Paul promised he'd help 'em
out.

"I think I can do it for you all right," he says. "I'll be up
tomorrow and look over the job."

But when Paul come up and see what a haywire outfit they
was tryin' to do the excavatin' with he was sure pretty near

plum digusted.

"Ain't you got a plow and a scraper?" he says.

"No. Elliott's badgers and catapults is all we got," they says. "Exceptin' some mules and single harness—and we got a six-tooth harrow."

"I got the Bay pretty near dug with my catapults, though," says Mr. Elliott.

"The Bay ain't but just big enough for you to put your name on it," says Old Man Puget.

"I'll send to my friend, Andrew Carnegie, for a plow and a scraper for your job," says Paul. "He can probly make one back there in Pittsburgh."

It took Carnegie's whole output of steel for the last year and six months to make them implements Paul ordered for the company and it took sixteen Mogul engines to ship 'em across the country.

But even after all that bother and after pretty near a perfectly good whole week of waitin' they wasn't half or even quarter big enough, and Paul couldn't use 'em. The plow went down only forty foot or so the deepest it could be set, and the scraper couldn't only carry but about 408 ton at a time.

Paul was thinkin' for a minute and then, like always, he got an idea.

"What's the matter with me?" he says. "Why ain't I thought of it before? There's glaciers up in Alaska that can dig lakes and rivers and sounds and valleys and anything else you've a mind to. I'll go up and get one of them."

And so he gets Babe and goes up there to Alaska and hitches onto one of the biggest of them glaciers up there and brings it down, and then he goes ahead to plow out the Sound.

Naturally he didn't need no scraper, because that glacier hadn't been used to havin' a scraper workin' behind it anyhow and could do the whole process in one swipe by itself, the way it'd always done up in Alaska all them thousands of years. And so it didn't take Paul long to dig the Sound.

One day when Paul was plowin', Babe shied at a school teacher with a pink parasol, and started to run away. Paul dug his heel into the ground to stop the Ox, and that's how Hood's Canal happened to be made. But he got him stopped before he got quite through, and he never bothered to go back there again, and so it's never been quite finished.

Babe shouldn't of scared that way—it wasn't nothin' to be

afraid of—only Old Dad Hood's daughter on her way home
from school—but that was the first umbrella he'd ever seen,
and he never could abide pink anyhow.

I should of mentioned before now, I guess, that Babe'd
growed kind of ornery and queer since he'd come out to the
Coast. It was the feed that didn't agree with him, I know.
That was the principal reason, except the hotcakes, of course.
But Douglas fir tops ain't exactly the right kind of fare and
not as good as what he'd always been used to havin' back in
Dakota and Wisconsin—clover hay, and baled timothy, and
redtop.

The alfalfa that Paul tried to raise for him had all been
drowned out the fall before by the yellow rain that had come
up from China—between the two of 'em, the dry Washington rain comin' down from on top and the yellow Chinese rain
comin' up from below, it was too much for the alfalfa hay,
and soaked the roots all out and killed it dead.

I never understood about that Chinese rain. It don't seem
reasonable that rain should come up from down there that
way, but we couldn't see how the ground could ever get that
wet from any ordinary rain from on top, and so we figgured
it must of been a Reverse rain like that, that done it—or
helped, anyway.

Paul thought he'd try to make up to Babe for the hay he
was missin' by feedin' him Shredded Wheat Biscuit baled up
with haywire, but Babe knowed that he wasn't gettin' nothin'
but wind and turned it down flat, and I don't know as I blame
him any; I know I would of done the same thing if I'd been
him.

And all the time, of course, he was gettin' more and more

AND THAT'S HOW HOODS CANAL HAPPENED TO BE MADE

vicious, and more and more crazy for them hotcakes, that he'd got such a habit for, and you couldn't hardly keep 'em away from him no more.

He got so ornery he just struck flat one day when Paul was plowin' down near Olympia.

Paul stopped and fuddled around a while to plant some oysters so's the govenor would always have some fresh for his table when he was entertainin' govenors from other states, and I guess maybe the Ox thought he was monkeyin' around too long. Anyway when Paul come back to go on and drive on further, Babe wouldn't move a step.

I guess you know Paul'd meant to connect up the Sound with the Columbia River and so make a complete job of it, but on account of that balky streak of Babe's that day it ain't never got done. Paul was about as mad as he ever was at Babe, but no sir, he couldn't make the Ox move an inch.

Anyway it was a pretty good Sound, Paul thought, and fulfilled all the specifications, except probly it was a little rough and uneven around the edges where he'd tried to scratch around a little at first with that plow Carnegie'd made for him. He could of smoothed that out, I spose, and straightened it up, but what's the use? Seattle real estate men would have more frontage on the Sound to sell if he didn't, he figgured, and then besides he had a job at Bellingham too that he wanted to start in on as soon as he could.

The city council of Bellingham had wanted a Bay for Bellingham for a long time so's the ships could come closer up to the wharves and not have to sail up on dry land, and they sent down to Paul and asked him to dig a bay for 'em while he was at it, and they'd be willin' to pay him extra for his trouble, they said.

Well, Paul went up there, but right in the spot where he wanted to put the bay, an old homesteader by name of Baker had took up a homestead, and he wouldn't get out of the way or sell or do nothin'.

Paul tried for pretty near two weeks to get the old man to change his mind and he even hired one of them there lawyers that can talk backwards and forwards at the same time to talk to him for him, but he wouldn't budge, and then one day Paul got mad, and they had a real row.

About two weeks after that when old man Baker got out of the hospital, Bellingham Bay was all done.

Paul just happened to meet the old man on the street one day.

"There's your farm," he says to him. "I put the dirt all up there on the other side of the town for you. And you can name it for yourself if you want to."

And so that's how Mount Baker got its name.

Old Man Puget and his partners, Elliott, and Rainier, and Hood, as soon as they'd collected their money from the goverment, went up to settle with Paul, but they didn't like to part with the money they'd got very well, and they was goin' to try to jew him down if they could.

Well, Paul he just stands there with one foot on either side of Deception Pass and lets 'em talk for a while, and then after a while he just calmly takes up his shovel and picks up a shovelful of dirt from the east side of the Sound and throws it out in the water, kind of as if he wasn't thinkin' about what he was doin'. Well, and then as they goes on talkin' and tryin' to explain to him that seein' it didn't take him as long as they'd expected it to take him, they'd rather pay him so much a day, and that would be fair, instead of payin' him for the whole job, and goes on that way, all of 'em together, Paul he just picks up another shovelful and another shovelful, and another shovelful, and without lookin' at 'em or payin' no attention to 'em, throws 'em into the Sound.

Well, when they seen all of a sudden what he was aimin' to do, and if they didn't pay him right away, he'd soon have the whole Sound filled up again, they run right for the money-sack and paid him quick, I can tell you.

You would think they would of learned their lesson the other time, when they sent him a carload of cheap tobacco—Paul just begun shovelin' dirt back in the Sound, till some clerk reported to 'em what he was doin' and they sent him a carload of good tobacco and an apology quick, I can tell you. But they didn't seem to've remembered that till next time.

Them shovelfuls of dirt that Paul throwed back in the Sound is the San Juan Islands now. Since they've got over-grown with trees and rocks and blackberry vines they've come to be mighty pretty to look at. But of course they're in the way of the ships a little bit, them that are goin' to Victoria.

Some says that a long time ago Paul dug the Pacific Ocean, too, the same as he dug the Sound, but that's just a story that's grown up, I think—the way stories will. A story seems to get started and then keeps on goin' till nobody knows where it first come from.

Old Mr. Pacific's own grandchildren officially denied the rumor here in court a couple of years ago. Paul didn't have nothin' to do with the Pacific Ocean—not directly anyway.

Indirectly, of course—he's indirectly responsible for its bein' salt.

The way that was:

Where they used to soak out the salt pork for the beans in the sink in Paul's camp in Oregon, the drainage from the sink where they soaked out the pork run down and made the ocean salt. And then you can see the foam on the waves yet too, that comes from the soapsuds they used in the big nets in the river where they rinsed off the knives and spoons.

CLEARING THE LA CONNER FLATS

AUL didn't get to go back to his loggin' for very long after he'd finished the Puget Sound job. In fact, he didn't hardly get to go back at all. For it was just about that time that the Tacoma people begun botherin' the life out of him to move the Mountain for 'em.

You know the way that was—like I said before—what was planned in the first place, before they started diggin' even —that Mountain should of been named for Tacoma. But a nephew of Mr. Rainier, that was a lawyer, had drawed up the contract, and he'd put it in the contract that the Mountain should be named for his uncle, Mr. Rainier, who'd been an admiral when he was a young fellow. And so now when they wanted to change it, there wasn't nothin' the goverment could do about it. And that's why Tacoma wanted Paul to move it inside their City Limits. A fellow always wants to watch out for them lawyers, for they're puttin' somethin' over all the time.

Well, and so then, though it wasn't no use, them Tacoma people was fussin' about it, and they thought Paul ought to move it for 'em. But Paul said he couldn't do it. He drawed the line on that. It's too bad he put it where he did, he said, and he was sorry all right, but it wasn't no fault of his, he was only obeyin' orders of Messrs. Puget, Hood and Company, and them Tacoma fellers should of been on the job at the beginnin'. No use kickin' afterwards. If they'd of told him at the time where to put it, he would of put it wherever they wanted, but he wasn't goin' to move it now. But he was willin' to do anythin' else they wanted him to, he told 'em, to oblige 'em, and that's how it come they hired him to make the Tacoma Prairies for an airplane base and an automobile race-track, just outside the city.

And another thing he made for 'em, and didn't charge 'em for, was the Stadium. He built that first for a corral for Babe, but it wasn't anywheres near big enough for the Ox, and so he just left it there for the city of Tacoma, and it's made a mighty fine Stadium, and one that's made Seattle jealous ever since.

Paul come pretty near bein' arrested when he was on that prairie job. And it was like this: seems that part of the land they was goin' to use was reserved and they didn't have no proper kind of permit for clearin' it.

But the goverment inspectors didn't get Paul, though, and that's because of the side-hill fall that him and Red Jack had practiced up on back in Michigan.

You see, trees growin' on a side-hill is pretty hard to fall, because you can't hardly tell where they're goin' to when you fall 'em, and so Paul and Red Jack had practiced up a lot on 'em when they was back on the Pyramid, in Michigan. Finally they got so they could make 'em go just where they wanted to, one on top of the other, or the other on top of the first one, or one right on the stump of another, or criss-cross like a ladder, a whole lot of 'em together, or anythin'; and so here on the level it wasn't nothin'—after they'd been used to the side-hill.

So what they done when they was clearin' the Tacoma Prairies was, they'd always fall one tree on the stump of another tree and knock it down in the ground, and that way they never had but one tree down at a time that could be used as evidence against 'em.

So when the investigation was on and them inspectors come along all they found was one tree down, and they reported back to the goverment:

"Said Paul Bunyan ain't been stealin' no timber. All he's got is one tree, and everywhere to one side of this tree is nothin' but prairie."

So that way Paul could of made the Prairies as big as they'd a mind to of had 'em, but the Tacoma people was scrappin' over the Mountain yet, and they thought the Prairie was big enough now, and so Paul quit when he'd finished as much of it as there is now, and then he went up and helped the La Conner people clearin' their Flats.

That was kind of a mean job, though, and kind of dirty, because they'd had a flood on the Skagit River just before he come up, and the mud up there hadn't no bottom to it.

Paul sunk in pretty near up over his ears, and Babe sunk in so deep Paul was afraid he would go clean through to

China, for only the brass tips on his horns was showin' above the mud sometimes. It was goin' to be a pretty tough job clearin' land in that there kind of country, and Paul seen he was goin' to have to do somethin' so they wouldn't sink in so far.

And so then Paul used his brain, like he generally done.

Well, I don't know what I would of done under them circumstances, but I can tell you what Paul done, after he'd been thinkin' for a while.

Remember them snowshoes I mentioned he was wearin' that first time he come out to Seattle, when he made the Grand Canyon? Well, that's what he used.

He'd cached 'em down in the State Museum when he found he couldn't use 'em no more, and now he went and got 'em again. And that give him the idea what to do for Babe too.

And so he just took a couple of logs and shaped 'em up like sled runners and nailed braces across 'em, and made mud-shoes for Babe, and they worked just fine. Afterwards they've used 'em for sleds for donkey engines. A few years ago somebody found one of Babe's shoes in a hole where the mud'd been, and picked it out and set his donkey engine on it, and that's what that kind of shoe is used for generally always now.

I guess it would make Babe pretty good and mad if he was here to see it—the way they do now. Them pesky donkey engines that he always hated so like sin, doin' all the favorite work he used to do, and drinkin' out of his rivers, and now wearin' his shoes even.

Paul used to water Babe in the Puyallup River while he was on the La Conner job. Babe used to drink the river dry for three miles up and down every time he was watered. One time he tried to drink it dry all the way down to the ocean because Paul'd lost his watch somewheres and wanted to know if by accident he might of dropped it in the river.

But he hadn't, though, as a matter of fact.

All the time it was in the bottom of Paul's loggin' pants, where he'd turned 'em up around the leg.

One time on one of the Oregon jobs Paul had Ole make him a donkey engine to use on part of the work. Ole made it one day, but the next mornin' when they got up, the donkey engine was gone, and the next mornin' the one he'd made that day was gone too, and so the next day when he made one, him and Paul made up their minds they was goin' to watch and see what become of it.

If there was anythin' in the world Paul hated to see it was petty thievin', and he wasn't goin' to have no camp thieves around his camp carryin' off any of his stuff—no matter what it was, donkey engines or anythin' else. And so he loaded up his gun with buckshot and salt and laid down by Ole behind a shed to see what was goin' to happen.

"We'll just give him a few where it'll do him the most good and I guess he'll know enough not to come prowlin' around my stuff any more," Paul says.

But nothin' happened till about midnight, and then they seen the door of Babe's barn come open.

"I thought the thief must of been hidin' in there," Paul says. But no thief come out; only the Blue Ox himself.

Ole and Paul watched to see where he was goin', and he walked right over to the open place where the new donkey engine stood, and they couldn't figgur out for the life of 'em what he was goin' to do there.

What he done was, he just picked up that there donkey on one horn and carried it into the barn, and into his stall. Paul and Ole followed after a while, and there under his crib in the hay they found all three of them there engines—he was just finishin' scrapin' a little hay over the one he'd just brought in there last to cover it up good.

Well, Paul he was always soft-hearted where the Ox was concerned, and that time his heart was touched if it ever was.

"I'll bust these donkey engines up and burn 'em tomorrow," he says to Ole. "I ain't goin' to use no more of them things, not on this job anyway. I guess I can manage with the cattle and the horse teams and the goats I got. Babe's always been a faithful Ox to me, and I ain't goin' to hurt his feelin's now at this time of life."

And so they didn't use the donkey engines on that job, and Ole's work for three days was gone for nothin', but that just shows how Babe felt about the new loggin' riggin' that was beginnin' to take his place. Poor old fellow. It was sure kind of hard on him.

Oh, yes, and I come pretty near forgettin'. One day when Paul was plowin' up on the La Conner Flats somethin' almost kind of funny happened.

I suppose everybody knows what cedar stumps are. And how tough they are. Well.

Well, Paul was plowin' one day on an afternoon late in the fall and he run right square plank into one of them there cedar stumps with his breakin' plow.

It was near sundown, and we was gettin' our cattle unyoked and gettin' ready for quittin' time, when all of a sudden we

AND THERE HE WAS, STUCK FAST

heard him holler and what's more, and certainly pretty funny for Paul—he was hollerin' for help. So we looked, and there he was, stuck in one of them cedar stumps.

And what'd happened was, he'd drove into the stump with his plow, and the stump had split down the middle and him and the plow had gone through, and then the old stump clamped together again, and there he was, stuck fast by the seat of his pants in the crack in the stump, and he couldn't get out no way.

So we went up there and hitched all our teams—about twenty of 'em in all—along with the Blue Ox, and pulled him out.

Only it didn't go as quick as that, because we was all fooled at first, and made a bad mistake.

There was a rise of ground out a ways from the stump, and a little hollow, and the way we had the teams yoked up at first, with Babe out ahead, we come near stranglin' all the other cattle.

"Look out! The cattle's all up in the air!" someone yelled, that was standin' off to the side, and we looked, and here, sure enough, they was all suspended up in the air and come pretty near havin' their heads yanked off.

You know the way it was, Babe was up on a hill, and when he give a pull, the others was just naturally lifted right off their feet and come pretty near all bein' strangled.

Well, then we unhooked 'em again and yoked 'em up the other way, Babe next to the plow, Paul hangin' onto the handles of it, and the other smaller cattle up ahead.

Murphy had 'em all heave together at the same time, and so we got Paul out all right, and the old cedar stump come right out with him, roots and all.

But it was mighty hard on his suspenders, though. Pants held good, he said—he wasn't worried about them none, for they was real loggers' pants—but it was a considerable strain on his suspenders—that is why he hadn't said much durin' the performance, he told us afterwards, because he was worryin' about whether they was goin' to hold or not.

Yes, and another time Paul helped one of the ranchers up there a little with his house-movin'.

A fellow was goin' to build a house up on the hill at La Conner and it's kind of rocky up there and it would be awful hard to dig a cellar in the rock. So he asked Paul what he'd better do about it and Paul told him to go ahead and build the house down on the flats where the cellar would be easy to dig, and he'd haul it up for him with the Blue Ox, and that's what he done—hauled the whole nine-room house up first and then went back and hauled the cellar up afterwards.

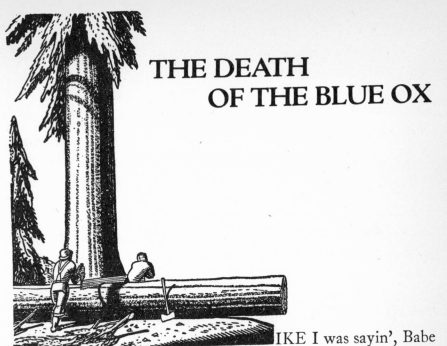

THE DEATH
OF THE BLUE OX

IKE I was sayin', Babe wasn't quite the same after he come out here to the Coast. I don't know what all got into him, but he got awful scrawny and thin after a while, and so touchy there wasn't hardly no gettin' along with him at all. And especially any time he couldn't get hotcakes, he was worse then, of course.

The habit for hotcakes had growed on him more and more all them years, and some of us pretty near knowed it was goin' to turn out bad in the end, but of course we didn't know it was goin' to be as bad as it was. For it'd got so there wasn't hardly no keepin' him away from 'em no more, and Paul, of course, didn't dare give him all he wanted.

If Brimstone Bill had only been there it wouldn't of been so bad, but Bill'd wore out at last and'd had to go and spend his last days with a sister he had somewheres down in Idaho, and the new fellow that was goin' to take care of Babe didn't use the right methods on him at all. Jake'd used to be a cow-puncher and them bronco-bustin' methods of his didn't do for Babe; and Paul couldn't hardly take the time to take care of him himself no more, with everything else he had to do—I don't really know as he ought to of tried to do all them things.

And anyway, I guess, maybe Babe got lonesome too—for the old Michigan winters and the snow and the sleddin' and all that, and he didn't like the climate out here very well—though it's supposed to be the best climate on earth. And then, like I said, the feed was poor too—Douglas fir tops ain't much to work hard on all day. It seems he was hungry pretty near all the time. And then, of course, I spose it was just a good part old age. Babe was gettin' pretty old for an Ox to've worked so hard all his life, like he'd done. But if Paul'd had good feed for him and enough of it, I know it would of been better, but he didn't, and that's what made Babe so greedy, I think.

If the boys would of knowed, back in Michigan, when they fed him hotcake-and-cloverhay sandwiches just for fun, that it was goin' to turn out like this they sure wouldn't of done it. But you can never tell about anything like that beforehand. Nobody couldn't hardly do anythin' with him no more.

One time he got into the honey Paul'd got out of the bee-tree that time he was huntin' bear, and got himself an awful toothache again and had to have the very last tooth he had left in his lower jaw pulled out and the one on the other side filled with copper plate.

It took an extra good kind of dentist and one trained for an acrobat too on account of Babe's mouth bein' so high, and with a couple of good helpers and some good rope ladders. The derrick they used in pullin' that last tooth was used for a stump puller afterwards, and they had to use steam hammers for the one they filled, next to it—and that reminds me, there ought to be a good copper mine somewheres in this country if anybody could only locate it.

And another time Babe swallowed eight rolls of barb wire that Paul was goin' to build a corral with, and he sure come pretty near killin' himself that time. Paul sent a kid in right away to cut up the wire in pieces so it wouldn't tie up his insides so bad and so's the pieces could work themselves out in time, but it was pretty near five months afterwards before the last of them pieces of wire come out through his hide. The last piece come out through a place along the right side of his back just back of the shoulder.

And once he pretty near killed himself overeatin' on cowfeed.

We was all in eatin' dinner that time and there wasn't nobody out there to watch Babe, and he got into a shed where somebody'd stored cowfeed—four whole bins of it—and he swallowed it all down at one time.

And, what always happens in them cases, he naturally swelled right up.

It wouldn't of been so bad, only Paul wasn't home at the time, and that made everybody all excited.

One of the buckers was the first to come out, and he seen what'd happened and begun hollerin' around, and run for the water bucket that was standin' by the door of the barn and give Babe a big drink of water. And then, naturally, that made him swell up all the worse.

Well, by that time most of the rest of us was out there too, and all excited.

"Where's a pitchfork?" hollers somebody. "Stick a pitch-fork into 'im. Quick! And let the air out of him."

"Get a pitchfork! Get a pitchfork!" everybody begins hollerin'.

But it just seems there wasn't no pitchfork around the place nowheres.

"Maybe a peavey'd do," somebody says.

"No, a peavey's got a hook on it, you fool," says somebody else. "And you wouldn't be able to get it out again."

And we sure thought we was goin' to have to stand there and look on when poor old Babe would bust right there before our eyes.

But just then somebody noticed one of the cookees with the dinnerhorn in his hand—he'd picked it up when he come runnin' out, and he was wavin' it like a wild man in the air.

So then Ole the Blacksmith grabs the horn from the flunky and sticks it into him, and the wind begun comin' out.

But the poor Ox got so scared when he heard the horn tootin', he just started on a run down the hill, and there wasn't no bridge over the river and he run right down into the drink, and we was all runnin' after him and the horn tootin' all the time like a Kansas thunderstorm. And then the water begun runnin' down the horn, and the poor old Ox begun to sink be-cause he was bein' drowned both on the outside and on the inside at the same time, and we sure thought he was a goner.

But just about that time the wind in his stomach must of begun comin' out again, because pretty soon we seen the water begin spurtin' out just like a geyser, and then it wasn't long till Babe floated up high enough so's we could get a rope around

SPURTIN' OUT JUST LIKE A GEYSER

his horns and get a block and tackle and haul him out.

But we sure was pretty excited for a while, for we would of hated to have somethin' like that happen to him—and specially while Paul was away and wasn't there to say what to do.

Then after he got home Paul built a corral for Babe up near Snoqualmie, so he'd have a place to keep him, because the forest inspector said he was eatin' up the spruce forest too fast. And that way Babe'd have a place to go in at night to lay down and rest for a while.

It was built of Douglas fir posts 70 foot high—raised up on end for a kind of stockade. But this corral wasn't no success, though, because the very first night Babe slept in it he busted it down—or the mornin' after the first night, I should of said.

He must of been sleepin' with his hind quarters pretty close up to the north wall and when he raised up in the mornin' first on his hind legs—like cattle always do, of course—and then on his front ones, why, his hind parts went right through the stockade and the whole thing fell down—and it wasn't no use tryin' to put it up again, because Paul knowed then it wouldn't never hold that way.

So the next time Paul built a corral, he made it of wire— because that would give in a similar case like that, he figgured.

He picked out a place where the tall trees was growin' pretty thick so he could just stretch the wire around from tree to tree, and he put them pretty close together up and down and around the corral, big enough so Babe would have room enough to turn around this time. He hired a telephone crew to build it for him, and it took 48 high climbers five weeks to put up the wire.

If Paul could of put up a corral big enough so's to've pervided enough grazin' ground inside, he might of saved Babe his last final death, I think, but I spose he couldn't do that.

What he done was, when his own spruce grazin' lands was pretty well gone, he turned Babe into the goverment forest reserves. Of course the forest ranger wouldn't stand for that, because that way they wouldn't have no forests for our children and grandchildren, he said, and so he ordered Paul to take him out and tie him along the outside edge of the forest —he could do that with goverment's permission, if he wanted to.

"He ain't used to bein' on a rope, and I don't know if he'd stay or not," Paul says.

"He'll just have to get used to it then," says the ranger, "like the rest of 'em."

"But I ain't got no rope strong enough to hold him," Paul says. "My Ox is a pretty strong Ox, you know."

"I can tell that by lookin' at him," says the ranger. "Maybe you could get a chain in town. I saw one out at the docks one day that looked pretty stout. Why don't you try one of them?"

Well, that give Paul an idea.

What he done was, he just went and bought back the big anchor chain from that ship he'd had when he carried lumber to Japan, and he tied the Ox with that to Mt. Pilchuck.

But he hadn't calculated just right anyway. It wasn't strong enough to hold. Well, that is, I guess the chain was strong enough all right—I don't believe that broke ever—but the mountain wasn't, you know.

One mornin' Babe got a whiff of hotcakes cookin' in a camp over in Vancouver, and then it was all off. On starvation rations like he'd been on for a couple of weeks, the smell of them hotcakes was too much for him. He just give one lunge and was off, and he tore the mountain loose and everythin', and just went likkity-split until he got there, and he didn't stop for nothin'.

The mountain come up with the chain and dragged along behind, but after a while Babe caught it on a stump or somethin' and it come off and he lost it, and that's why Mt. Pilchuck today is right where it is, instead of bein' a hundred or a hundred fifty miles further south where it used to be. That all come of that run that mornin'.

Babe got into the camp in Vancouver just as the cook was fryin' the last stove-top-full of hotcakes. It wasn't a very big camp, only about 400 men or so, and there wasn't an awful lot of hotcakes on hand, only about four platters stacked four foot high that the flunkies was just goin' to start down the tables with on the run, for the bell for breakfast was ringin' just then, when Babe busts into camp. The store-room back of the kitchen he laid out flat, and he took one jump over that, and then he made straight for the stove and the hotcake platters.

He swallowed all that was on the platters in just two swallows and a half, and then he made for them on the stove and he was so greedy he just swallowed the hotcakes, stove, fire, cook, hotcake turner and all in one swallow.

Well, the cook'd just filled the stove up with good dry spruce wood so's to have plenty of fire for the last batch of cakes, an' it had just got goin' good, and it burned Babe's insides out before anybody had time to do anythin' for him, an' everybody just stood and gawked. The blacksmith there, though, was just shoein' a donkey engine, an' he brought that in to pull the last painful breaths out of Babe's body, and so helped him out some.

Poor old Babe! Had a hard life the last few years of it, all right. And it must of been an awful death for him, too, but maybe after all, the way everythin' was, he was glad to quit.

They butchered the carcass, and the inside meat that was roasted enough by the fire inside him they canned up for canned roast beef that you can still see on the market, and the rest they packed in 240 refrigerator cars and sold to the different loggin' and minin' companies operatin' on the Sound afterwards.

Most of 'em got some of the Blue Ox meat left yet, I judge from the reports that comes in.

Just the other day a fellow come in here to ask what time the stage left and he stopped and talked to me a minute or two where I was settin' on the porch—for I guess he seen I was an old logger—and he happened to just mention that he'd been workin' in Lovell's Upper 7, and so I asked him how they was feedin' up there now. And he says "pretty punk— they got too much of that there Paul Bunyan meat on hand for good feedin'," he says. The roast meat they had the day before he quit, he said, must of been from the shoulder of the Ox, because it was so tough—where the yoke'd rubbed when he was haulin' them big loads back on the Pyramid Forty.

PAUL'S
LAST STAND

ELL, yes, Paul's gone now. And it's more than ten years now since I seen him last. He was off for Alaska then, he said, and I don't believe he's ever come back, and so I guess he's up there yet. They say he's loggin' by airplane now and that he's gettin' out timbers for the Mexican goverment to build their navy off. Some say they've seen his airplanes goin' across the sky on the way, fetchin' the timber down to Mexico. I don't know. I ain't never seen 'em myself. But I mean to watch out, though. Whatever he's doin', he's doin' somethin' big, you can bet your last nickel on that.

It just happened that I seen Paul the day he pulled off finally for Alaska. I happened to be down to the dock that day and so I seen him step aboard and got to say good-by to him. He went up on the old steamer *Queen* that used to run between here and Juneau in the old days.

"Well, he's dead, Angus," he says to me when I reached out my hand to shake hands with him just before he stepped aboard.

"Yes, I heard about it," I says.

Naturally, he was talkin' about the Ox. Paul was all broke up about the loss of the Ox, and I knowed that too. I'd heard the men talkin' about it, though I hadn't been workin' for him for the last couple of months.

Some of 'em said they didn't think he could ever get over it, and I don't know but what they was right.

"He was hungry," he says. "We ain't had the right feed for Babe for a long time. Babe was hungry, or he wouldn't of done it, I know."

"Yes, sure, he was hungry, Paul," I says, "or I don't think he would of done it." But I don't know as I believed that, for I'd watched his bad habit for hotcakes grow on him, and I pretty near knowed somethin' would of happened some day anyhow.

"I can't never do the loggin' I used to do, again," Paul says. "Not without Babe. He was a faithful Ox to me. I guess I'm gettin' old. I want to see the snow again and try some of the old-time loggin' once more."

Paul was feelin' pretty bad, I guess, about the way his loggin'd got broke up out here them last years.

"Good-by," I says. And then just to cheer him up a bit: "And good luck to you, like old times, Paul," I says.

"Same to you, Angus Campbell," he says, "good luck to you too, like old times."

And with that he reaches out his hand across the twenty-

PAUL WAS ALL BROKE UP

eight foot of water between us and gives my hand a hard
squeeze that I can feel yet sometimes when the wind is from
the north, and just about that minute the boat whistled, and
she sailed away, with Paul a-standin' there on the deck.

And that's the last I ever seen of him.

Oh, there's reports that's come through. Some say he's gone
up to the North Pole and that he's helped Santa Claus make
new sled runners and some other things for his annual business
trip South once a year, and some says he has the pole all rigged
up for high-lead loggin', and that he's loggin' off the Arctic
Circle. And some say that he's been back to the States a number of times, and that he's tried ranchin' down in Oregon,
raisin' an extra-extra big kind of apple, and that he's dry-
farmed over in Nevada, and had a cattle ranch down in Idaho
once again after that other time.

I don't know about cattle ranches. I don't believe he'd try
that again after the kind of luck he had the other time.

You know he did try dairy ranchin' once, when he thought
he was goin' to use cow milk in his camps instead of canned
cow. He bought a combination popcorn and dairy ranch and it
was a mighty fine one too. But in the fall when he had his popcorn all put up in granaries and his cattle all out grazin' on
the fall clover, somebody'd dropped a cigarette stub out near
the corncrib and set fire to the whole outfit. The popcorn all
popped at one time right away, and when the cows seen it
come spreadin' out all over the field and gettin' about three or
four foot thick they thought it was a Kansas blizzard and they
every last one of 'em froze to death before Paul had time to
drive 'em away from there or rake the popcorn out. So after

that experiment I don't believe he'd try anythin' like that again—especially after he lost Lucy too—that was Paul's favorite cow—she used to give so much milk it took seven men to skim the cream. One winter when the snow was extra deep she used to graze on the pine and balsam tops that was the only trees that was stickin' up above the snow and the milk was so strong that the men used to use it for cough syrup. And she had to roam so far to get enough fodder that Paul had to hang a church bell on her to keep her from gettin' lost. But she was with the rest of the herd out there in the popcorn blizzard that time and she froze to death just the same as the others.

Oh, there's all kinds of stories. There's one about a thrashin' outfit he had once when he was up in Alberta. I guess that must of been the time before he logged North Dakota when he used to get some of the supplies for his camp from his farm up there.

An Irishman by the name of Mike Flannery told me this story. I don't know as I can remember it, but I can see if I can—just for fun.

Mike says he and Paul started out together on that thrashin' outfit from Winnipeg, and they sent men ahead on horseback and motorcycles to let the farmers know they was comin', so they'd be ready for 'em.

They had a big Case outfit and the engine was so big it had eight fly-wheels and could run on either its bottom, side, or top, just as good. The belt was lengthened to four and one-fourth miles, because they didn't want to have no short sets, but when they was movin' they shortened it up a little of course, so as to give the quick-movin' device that Paul had invented a chanst. The quickest record of movin' they ever made,

Mike says, was one of thirty-nine miles from set to set, and it was done in exactly eleven and five-sixteenths seconds. The separator was equipped with automatic feeders and blowers that would blow the straw out on the fields again for fertilizer, and the engine was rigged up with a patent Bunyan condenser on the injector pipe that could take in water from the clouds, and also had a smokeless smokestack—improvements that was put in by Paul. The engine used 400 gallons of water an hour and 51 tons of coal, and could develop a horsepower of over forty-two thousand.

Well, the first thrashin' they done was for a farmer in Alberta. They'd stopped first in a wheatfield, but Paul wanted to thrash oats first, he said, so Ole, who was the champion pitcher and was pitchin' for Paul that fall, had to pitch the oats acrost three sections of wheat to toss it into the separator.

Just when they'd got good and started and before they'd thrashed more than about 2000 bushel or so, Howie—that's the farmer—come runnin' up to Paul and says for him to stop.

"There's a hen over on the separator that's starvin' to death," he yells. "Stop the machine so we can save her. Quick!"

Well, Paul he knowed what it was all right, but just to humor the fellow he stopped, and went over with the farmer to look at the hen.

"The poor thing looks as if she hasn't had a grain to eat since old man Noah let her out of the Ark," Howie says, and Paul he just laughed, because he knowed what it was, all right. The hen that Howie was feelin' sorry for was one that Paul and Mike had had painted on the separator for advertisin' to show what would happen to any hen that would try to pick a livin' off of the straw that come out of their machine.

Well, then Mr. Howie took the hen and fed her a couple of sackfuls of wheat and oats and took her in to his wife, and she laid three carloads of eggs that week—pretty near enough to feed the whole crew.

Durin' this trip Paul used to have to get sore at the pitchers a good many times because they wouldn't pitch the right kind of grain always—when he'd be callin' for wheat they'd be pitchin' barley, and when he'd be wantin' clover they'd be givin' him oats sometimes. And one time he got so mad at one of the kids, he threw him in the separator, boy, pitchfork, bundle of barley and all. But as luck would have it the blowers was pointed east on that set and the boy's home was in Boston and when he come out of the blower he was goin' at such speed that he landed up in Lowell, Massachusetts, where he found his brother in business conductin' a gents' furnishin' store. So it wasn't so bad for the kid after all.

About the end of the week Paul and Mike and the outfit caught up with the men on motorcycles that had been sent ahead, and waited over Sunday, so's to let 'em get ahead again and sign up some more contracts.

Ole took advantage of the Sunday lay-over to get good and gloriously drunk like old times.

It was early in the mornin' before the rest was up, and he went out and happened to run into a box car full of whisky standin' on the side-tracks. He broke into the car and drank up all the whisky and then he went to look for another carful to really get likkered up on, because the first one had only just made his appetite good for more.

He didn't find another whisky car, though, but a carload

of musical instruments instead, cornets and flutes and drums and fiddles and other things belongin' to a travelin' circus band, and Ole was just feelin' good enough from the little snack of whisky he'd had so he wanted to show off how good he could play, and he took one of the horns and started in to play some tune he'd learned in the old country when he was a boy but that he didn't remember so very well. I think it must of been that one about old man Noah they sing.

Anyway it woke Paul up, and Mike says he jumped out of bed right away to go out and see what that racket was, and there was Ole a-tootin' away at the horn as loud as he could— it was one of them there cornets he had.

"I bat you you cannint play so nice a tune like dat," says Ole.

And Paul he says, "I bet you I can, Ole."

And he takes the horn away from Ole and starts in to play.

But he didn't play no tune, though. For the very minute he started in, with his first breath of wind, that cornet straightened right out every last kink and curve in it straight up against the sky, and the noise it made was heard for 185 miles but it was only the one blast and you couldn't call that no tune, so Ole won the bet that time.

Paul finished his thrashin' in Canada just before Christmas and he and Mike sold out their outfit to an Italian named Pat Mahoney, who is still livin' on a ranch near Moosejaw, Mike says.

That young fellow Mike was sure a great talker, even for an Irishman.

Well, there's stories, and stories. I don't suppose I've heard 'em all. His old friends all remember him, and any of 'em will tell you about Paul. And some of 'em wishes a good many times that he was back here loggin' again; even the young fellows who never knowed him, but have only just heard about him, would of liked pretty well to've been in on the good old times, I guess.

I remember one young fellow that was caught under a car-load of logs up here in the pass a couple of years ago where I was workin', where it'd tipped over against the bank and pinned him under and mashed both his legs to a pulp and was holdin' him there tight so he couldn't move at all. And it was a couple of hours before they could get enough men together to help him out of there.

"I bet all the while you was layin' here," one of 'em says to him afterwards, "you was wishin' mighty hard that some of us would hurry and come along and get this timber off of you."

"No," he says. "That wasn't what I was wishin' at all. I wasn't worryin' about the timber none. What I was wishin' was that Paul Bunyan would come along with his old Blue Ox and hitch him onto this mountain and pull it out from under me. That's what I was wishin' all the time."

And it's times like them, or when a tree is goin' to be falled that's so crooked no mortal can tell which way it'll go, or maybe when a bragger comes to camp that thinks he knows more than the next fellow, and has to be took down a peg, or maybe when everythin' about the whole outfit goes haywire all at the same time, it's then that they remember Paul Bunyan and begin to talk about what he could do if he was there; and how he used to hew with that big ax of his, on the wove grass handle, and how he could twist the biggest tree around and make it fall where he wanted it to, and how in the old days he used to hitch Babe onto anythin' in sight, a whole section of timber even, and haul it down to the river ready for the Big Drive in the spring. And then they talk about North Dakota. For North Dakota, of course, was the biggest loggin' Paul ever done.

ACKNOWLEDGMENTS

Stewart and Watt, "Legends of Paul Bunyan," an article published in the annual publications of the Wisconsin Academy of Arts, Sciences and Letters for 1916, advertising booklets put out by the Red River Lumber Company of Minneapolis, and a chap-book, "Paul Bunyan Comes West," published by the University of Oregon (narrative by Ida Virginia Turney of the Department of English), have been examined for material for this compilation, and also the Paul Bunyan letters published in the *Seattle Star*, the *Portland Oregonian* and the *4L Bulletin*. My husband, C. Ellis Shephard, has helped me in collecting these stories. A great many friends have assisted in making the book, either by contributing stories or giving suggestions. Among those to whom I am particularly indebted are: Mr. Joe Mawhinnie of the British Columbia Timberworkers' Union, Vancouver, B. C.; Mr. W. J. Chambers of Clear Lake, Wash.; Mr. Charles O. Olsen of Portland, Ore.; Mr. B. C. Saterbo of Vashon, Wash.; Mr. W. B. Laughead, advertising manager of the Red River Lumber Company; Mr. E. S. Shepard of Rhinelander, Wis.; Mr. P. S. Lovejoy of Ann Arbor, Mich.; Mr. Carl Sandburg; Mr. DeWitt Harry of the *Portland Oregonian*; Prof. Edmond S. Meany, Prof. Victor Farrar and Prof. Leslie Spier of the University of Washington; Mr. Carl Van Doren; and Prof. V. L. O. Chittick of Reed College.

ESTHER SHEPHARD